Narrative Nursing - What Does it Mean to be a Professional Nurse

A nursing narrative note is a type of nursing documentation used to provide clear, detailed information about a patient. A narrative note is written in paragraph form and tells a story, if you will, about the patient, the care being received, response to treatment, and any interventions or education provided. Narrative notes allow for more detailed descriptions of health conditions and concerns, which means you have greater freedom when it comes to painting a representative picture of a patient's health. You can communicate their thoughts and feelings, as well as your own professional judgments.

The format of the book will cover the Narrative Nursing workshop format that has been instituted over the years with nurses from a range of organizations. Each nurse will follow an outline of storytelling and select one meaningful nurse-patient, nurse-colleague, or nurse-leader encounter to present as a story to share with other nurses. Each chapter contains stories from nurses at all levels of development, from the novice (student nurse) to the expert nurse and nurse leader.

The overall purpose is to illustrate, in a structured format, the impact of nursing care provided to individuals, families, and communities. The storytelling process that will be used includes the key techniques of storytelling: namely, engaging the audience, describing the scene, building tension, focusing on what is important, keeping the flow logical, and making the story conclusive, particularly in light of the lessons learned from the story. Each story will be accompanied by analysis and commentary from the two primary authors, remarking on the meaningfulness of the story, lessons learned, and lessons for other nurses.

Each story will be unique, but there will be conclusions drawn at the end of each story, and there will also be an introductory chapter and a final chapter written by the primary authors to introduce the value of story-telling and in the final chapter to synthesize lessons learned. A main feature of this book is that the stories will allow the reader to identify personal and professional moral and ethical principles confronted by clinical nurses and nurse leaders at all levels.

Narrative Nursing - What Does it Mean to be a Professional Nurse

Stories From the Field

Joyce J. Fitzpatrick and Peter Stoffan

Routledge
Taylor & Francis Group
A PRODUCTIVITY PRESS BOOK

Designed cover image: Shutterstock

First published 2026
by Routledge
605 Third Avenue, New York, NY 10158

and by Routledge
4 Park Square, Milton Park, Abingdon, Oxon, OX14 4RN

Routledge is an imprint of the Taylor & Francis Group, an informa business

ISBN: 978-1-032-95781-4 (hbk)
ISBN: 978-1-032-95089-1 (pbk)
ISBN: 978-1-003-58654-8 (ebk)

DOI: 10.4324/9781003586548

Typeset in Garamond
by Deanta Global Publishing Services, Chennai, India

Contents

Preface ix
About the Authors xi

1 Introduction to Narrative Nursing and Its Relationship to Professional Nursing Practice **1**
Why Is Storytelling Important in Nursing? 2
Philosophical Underpinnings of Nursing 4
Ways of Knowing in Nursing 4
The Role of Emotional Intelligence in Nursing 7
Benner's Model of Knowing in Clinical Nursing 7
Relationship to Quality and Safety Education for Nurses (QSEN) Competencies 10
Benner's Model for Nursing Knowledge Development 11
Summary of the Benner Model 13
NCLEX-RN Integrated Processes Categories 13
References 13

2 Caring: Introduction **15**
Caring: Novice 17
Reflection 22
Caring Narrative: Beginner 25
Reflection 30
Caring Narrative: Competent 33
Reflection 35
Caring Narrative: Proficient 37

Reflection....39
Caring Narrative: Expert....43
Reflection....45

3 Clinical Judgment: Introduction....47
Clinical Judgment: Novice....49
Reflection....51
Clinical Judgment: Beginner....53
Reflection....55
Clinical Judgment Narrative: Competent....59
Reflection....61
Clinical Judgment: Proficient....63
Reflection....64
Clinical Judgment: Expert....67
Reflection....71
References....73

4 Communication and Documentation: Introduction....74
Communication and Documentation Narrative: Novice....79
Reflection....82
Communication and Documentation Narrative: Beginner....85
Reflection....87
References....89
Communication and Documentation Narrative: Competent....91
Reflection....93
Communication and Documentation Narrative: Proficient....95
Reflection....96
Communication and Documentation Narrative: Expert....99
Reflection....101

5 Culture and Spirituality: Introduction 103
Culture and Spirituality Narrative: Novice 107
Reflection 111
Culture and Spirituality Narrative: Beginner 115
Reflection 117
Culture and Spirituality: Competent 119
Reflection 121
Culture and Spirituality: Proficient 123
Reflection 125
References 126
Culture and Spirituality: Expert 127
Lessons Learned and Recommendations 132
Reflection 134

6 Nursing Process: Introduction 136
References 138
Nursing Process Narrative: Novice 139
Reflection 140
Nursing Process Narrative: Beginner 143
Reflection 145
Nursing Process Narrative: Competent 147
Reflection 149
References 150
Nursing Process Narrative: Proficient 151
Reflection 156
Nursing Process Narrative: Expert 159
Reflection 163
References 164

7 Teaching and Learning: Introduction 165
Teaching and Learning Narrative: Novice 169
Reflection 172
Teaching and Learning Narrative: Beginner 175
Reflection 177
Teaching and Learning Narrative: Competent 179
Reflection 181

Teaching and Learning Narrative: Proficient 183
Reflection 186
Teaching and Learning Narrative: Expert 187
Reflection 189

8 Other Narratives from Professional Leaders at the Bedside and Beyond 190
Additional References 209

Index 213

Preface

This book is a celebration of nursing, sharing professional stories of the joys and challenges of professional nursing practice. It is a testament to the power, intelligence, humanity, and resilience and resourcefulness of nurses everywhere, in direct care, in leadership positions leading other nurses, and in the academic community. We have written this book because we love the work that we do as nurses, but most especially because we want to inspire future generations of nurses. We believe that our profession, as the most trusted and ethical profession, is not well understood by the public and is often not well understood within the health care arena.

This book can be used to help students and new graduates prepare for the NCLEX-RN licensure exam. At the same time, the book can be useful to several other groups of nurses, including those who want to reenergize their nursing career and those who are embarking on a new phase of their nursing career, whether a new position or a new specialty, or advanced education. Nurses' stories are a significant way to share our legacy as professional nurses dedicated to serving humanity and advancing global health.

Nurses remember the significant experiences in their professional lives through the stories they tell. Nurses learn from each other through stories, whether it is the senior nurse on the unit orienting new nurses or the clinical preceptor instructing the senior student. All in all, nurses' stories serve as a learning tool.

Even now, as nurses who have been part of the profession for decades, we, the editors, have learned from the stories shared by new and experienced nurses. We acknowledge each of the nurses who have shared their stories. We are indebted to them for their transparency regarding the lessons learned throughout their careers and the lessons that they are continuing to learn.

As authors of the primary content and editors of the stories, we are indebted to the nurses who shared their stories and their challenges.

Thank you, nurses!

About the Authors

Joyce J. Fitzpatrick, PhD, MBA, RN, FAAN, FNAP, FAANP(H), is the Director of the Marian K. Shaughnessy Nurse Leadership Academy and the Elizabeth Brooks Ford Professor of Nursing at the Frances Payne Bolton School of Nursing, Case Western Reserve University (CWRU) in Cleveland, Ohio, where she was Dean from 1982 through 1997. She is also a Distinguished University Professor at CWRU. She earned a BSN from Georgetown University, an MS in Psychiatric-Mental Health Nursing from the Ohio State University, a PhD in Nursing from New York University, and an MBA from CWRU. In 1990, Dr Fitzpatrick received an honorary doctorate, Doctor of Humane Letters, from Georgetown University. In 2011, she received an honorary doctorate, Doctor of Humane Letters, from the Frontier University of Nursing, and in 2020, she was appointed a Distinguished University Professor at CWRU.

Dr Fitzpatrick is widely published in nursing and health-care literature, with over 400 publications, including more than 85 books. She has received the AJN Book of the Year Award 22 times. She served as Co-editor of the *Annual Review of Nursing Research* series, vols. 1–26. She is the Editor of the classic *Encyclopedia of Nursing Research*, now in its 4th edition, and Co-editor of the *Encyclopedia of Nursing Education*. In 2021, with Dr Mary Beth Modic, she published a children's book titled *Luminaries of the Past: Stories of Fifty Extraordinary Nurses*.

Peter Stoffan, DNP, MPA, RN, CCRN, NEA-BC, CPXP, is a Nurse Leader currently residing in the New York City Greater Metro Area. Prior to Nursing, Peter earned his first-degree from Indiana University in Musical Theatre. After performing for multiple years in New York City and around the country, he decided to go back to school for Nursing at New York University. Peter loves the leadership role both on and off stage and enjoys blending the two dynamic talents in healthcare and leadership. After earning a Master's in Public Administration degree from New York University, he earned his Doctor of Nursing Practice (DNP) degree at Case Western Reserve University's Frances Payne Bolton School of Nursing. His scholarly work focuses on the connection between hospital and environmental attributes and the health of nurse leaders.

He has served in various leadership roles in healthcare organizations in the New York City Greater Metro Area and is adjunct faculty at the Frances Payne Bolton Schol of Nursing. Peter is also a published author of *Tommy the Nurse* – a children's book that highlights nursing and the importance of following one's own passions. Additionally, Dr Stoffan has written and edited book chapters, has articles published in the *Gastroenterology Nursing Journal, Nursing Management Journal,* and the *American Nurse Journal,* and is a contributing author for the book *Luminaries of the Past: Stories of Fifty Extraordinary Nurses*, written by Dr Joyce Fitzpatrick and Dr Mary Beth Modic.

Chapter 1

Introduction to Narrative Nursing and Its Relationship to Professional Nursing Practice

Stories make us human. We make sense of our universe and our lives through the stories that we tell ourselves about our experiences. We weave each of our interactions with the world into an understandable whole, one that is uniquely our own. We interpret our past as a story of our own making of reality, sometimes changing the facts so that they make sense to us and how we experience reality. We dream of our future and tell ourselves the stories that we want to make part of our future. Through goal setting around our stories, we can create our future reality. Storytellers, each of us, create moments of change. We interpret reality as change agents, creating understandings of the external world in order to make sense of it. And our interpretations are shaped by each of our

DOI: 10.4324/9781003586548-1

experiences. Our experiences in the world, the stories we tell ourselves in our interpretations of the world, are shaped by our cultural mores. And so it is with the interpretation of our nursing world, understanding all of our experiences through the nursing lens. As nurses, we believe that we are always on call as professionals, viewing all of our human experiences through our nursing lens. Throughout life, we think as nurses and act as nurses. Being a professional nurse is part of our being in the world. We cannot walk by another human without thinking about the health of that individual, wondering what we could do to make their lives better, healthier.

Why Is Storytelling Important in Nursing?

We have implemented storytelling through Narrative Nursing workshops and within a wide range of leadership development classes over the past several years. These experiences capture the essence of professional nursing, eliciting experiences that capture the interpersonal connection that nurses have with their patients and the professional influence that nurses have on the individual's health and well-being. Also, importantly, storytelling empowers nurses to understand their influence, leading care at the bedside for patients and families. We have found that there is a positive dimension to nurses sharing stories of nurse-patient relationships at the point of care. Nurses help each other understand the critical role that each plays in the care of patients. Nurses' stories are empowering, helping each nurse understand the value that they bring to the patient encounter and to the entire health care team. Sharing this value provides peer support for nurses and assists them in developing and maintaining an effective care team. Further, the stories of nurses and their patient encounters elucidate the critical role of the nurse-patient relationship, the essence of professional nursing. The connections that the nurse develops with patients and their families are essential to the patient's journey toward health.

Nursing professionals form a unique cultural group. No matter where you might find yourself in the world, nurses understand each other, including the day-to-day clinical experience of being a nurse, and the cultural components within the healthcare systems and communities in which nurses work. Nurses share a common language of the care that they provide, and although there may not be a formal linguistic taxonomy of nursing language, there is a shared understanding of the knowledge and practice of nursing. And there is a shared professional culture of what it means to be a nurse and think and act like a nurse.

There is a professional value in sharing our stories so that society (the public) understands the knowledge that nurses have about holistic health and the work that nurses do. As professionals, leading care at the bedside and throughout the communities in which they live and work, professional nurses serve as patient advocates and as champions of health care for all. Through storytelling, nurses share their collective community, both within and outside of the profession, a sense of shared purpose that is present through the educational preparation of professional nurses.

Nurses learn to "think like a nurse," a process that Caputi (2021) describes as the nurses' role in displaying both clinical reasoning (the thinking part) and clinical judgment (acting like a nurse). According to Caputi, nurses integrate their clinical judgment skills (noticing, interpreting, problem recognition, responding, evaluating/reflecting) through the nursing process and act accordingly. And throughout the process of becoming a professional, they capture their professional stories, learning from their experiences and sharing with the next generation of nurses.

Philosophical Underpinnings of Nursing

The holistic nature of nursing is reflected in the metaparadigm concepts: person, environment, health, and nursing that serve as the philosophical basis for the discipline. Within the context of these core constructs, the holistic nature of both nursing knowledge and nursing interventions is defined. The person is seen as contiguous with their environment, internal and external, physiological, psychological, sociological, cultural, and spiritual, but not as a collection of parts, but as an integrated whole. The outcome of nursing practice is health, not just the absence of disease, but rather the experience of wellness and well-being.

Ways of Knowing in Nursing

In 1978, Carper described fundamental patterns of knowing in nursing that integrated the scientific/theoretical and the practical/clinical ways of knowing. She framed these as interdependent, not distinct patterns of how professional nursing knowledge is developed. The patterns of knowing described by Carper include empiric, esthetic, ethical, and personal knowing.

Empirical knowing: the science of nursing, including research and evidence-based practice.

Esthetic knowing: the art of nursing; empathy and creativity in clinical practice; understanding deep meanings.

Ethical knowing: encompasses the moral values underlying nursing and is reflected in the professional codes of ethics developed through the professional nursing organizations at the national level, the American Nurses Association (ANA), and at the global level, the International Council of Nurses (ICN).

All professional nurses are guided by the ANA (2025) Code of Ethics for Nurses, which charts the course of ethical professional behavior and serves as the foundation for the contract that professional nurses have with society. The Code of Ethics is the definitive standard for ethical nursing practice used to guide nurses as they make patient care and practice decisions in complex healthcare environments. Professional nursing practice is also governed by the respective state-level legislative and regulatory policies of the states in which the nurse is licensed.

There are ten provisions included in the 2025 ANA Code of Ethics. These include the following:

Provision 1: The nurse practices with compassion and respect for the inherent dignity, worth, and unique attributes of every person.

Provision 2: A nurse's primary commitment is to the recipient(s) of nursing care, whether an individual, family, group, community, or population.

Provision 3: The nurse establishes a trusting relationship and advocates for the rights, health, and safety of recipient(s) of nursing care.

Provision 4: Nurses have authority over nursing practice and are responsible and accountable for their practice consistent with their obligations to promote health, prevent illness, and provide optimal care.

Provision 5: The nurse has moral duties to self as a person of inherent dignity and worth, including an expectation of a safe place to work that fosters flourishing, authenticity of self at work, and self-respect through integrity and professional competence.

Provision 6: Nurses, through individual and collective effort, establish, maintain, and improve the ethical environment of the work setting that affects nursing care and the well-being of nurses.

Provision 7: Nurses advance the profession through multiple approaches to knowledge development, professional standards, and the generation of policies for nursing, health, and social concerns.

Provision 8: Nurses build collaborative relationships and networks with nurses, other healthcare and non-healthcare disciplines, and the public to achieve greater ends.

Provision 9: Nurses and their professional organizations work to enact and resource practices, policies, and legislation to promote social justice, eliminate health inequities, and facilitate human flourishing.

Provision 10: Nursing, through organizations and associations, participates in the global nursing and health community to promote human and environmental health, well-being, and flourishing (ANA, 2025).

Galinas (2025) described the important elements of the 2025 revised Code of Ethics for Nurses as important in enhancing professional nursing through patient-centered care, advocacy, professional responsibility, ethical decision-making, and self-care. In addition, this new Code includes the profession's responsibility for global health and wellness.

In the global health arena, the nursing profession is guided by the International Council of Nurses (ICN) Code of Ethics. ICN is the global organization that represents nurses and nursing in more than 130 countries. The ICN Code of Ethics provides ethical guidance in relation to nurses' roles, duties, responsibilities, behaviors, professional judgment, and relationships with patients, others receiving nursing care or services, coworkers, and allied professionals (ICN, 2025).

Personal knowing: understanding of self; interpersonal relationships as a vehicle of nursing practice; value of humanity; value of connections within the global community toward health. Personal knowing has as a foundation knowledge and appreciation of the World Health Organization (WHO) definition of health: "Health is a state of complete physical, mental and social well-being and not merely the absence of disease or infirmity" (WHO, 2025).

The Role of Emotional Intelligence in Nursing

Emotional intelligence plays an important role in personal and professional success in nursing as well as in other professions and with individuals in their personal lives. Daniel Goleman (2005) outlines the five essential elements of emotional intelligence: self-awareness, self-regulation, motivation, empathy, and social skills. Learning how to cultivate and apply these components allows us to better navigate interpersonal dynamics, defuse conflicts, build fulfilling relationships, and thrive at work. As they develop their expertise in clinical practice, professional nurses concomitantly develop emotional intelligence skills. The holistic nature of thinking like a nurse, at the same time, practicing from a holistic framework, can enhance the clinical practice skills of the nurse. As professional nurses develop skills as outlined in the proficiency framework of Benner (1984), the nurses' emotional intelligence is also enhanced.

Benner's Model of Knowing in Clinical Nursing

Benner proposed that nurses gain knowledge through their understanding of the clinical practice of nursing. In other words, their knowledge is embedded in clinical experience and is gained over time through experiential learning. Nursing knowledge is developed, expanded, and synthesized through clinical experiences. Further, nurses' clinical experiences help them to move through the stages of knowing: from novice to expert. As nurses gain knowledge through their clinical experience, they learn how to be a nurse, a learning that is essential to their professional practice and their social contract with society.

Benner's model of understanding nursing clinical practice is directly related to the patterns of knowing, the ways in which nurses come to develop knowledge, as Carper described. This model requires the nurse to demonstrate perceptual awareness. To carry out the nursing roles that Benner describes requires the nurse to use the empiric, aesthetic, ethical, and personal ways of knowing described by Carper (1999). These roles also require that the nurse develop emotional intelligence, an awareness of one's total environment, and the role of self within that environment.

Within the Benner model, six domains of nursing practice are described. These include the following roles for professional nurses.

The **helping role** includes a wide range of initiatives implemented by professional nurses. The professional nurse creates a climate for healing, maximizes the individual's participation in their own recovery and journey through health, provides emotional and informational support, and helps the individual develop and implement goals that lead to health. Further, the professional nurse builds and maintains a therapeutic community with the individual, group, or community that is served.

Through the **teaching/coaching role,** the professional nurse assesses the individual's readiness to learn and times the interventions based on this assessment. The nurse elicits the individual's understanding of their illness and helps them to interpret their experiences in order to achieve a higher level of health. This is consistent with the description of the nurse's role in the story theory posited by Smith and Liehr (2005), in which the meaning of the health experience of the patient is the first assessment for the nurse. Once the patient/individual describes their interpretation of the illness, the nurse adds to this understanding with additional knowledge regarding health, illness, and well-being. The nurse serves as a coach to the individual recipient of care.

The **diagnostic role** of the nurse leads the nurse to identify key signs and symptoms that would be manifested with specific health challenges. For example, if the patient is a newly diagnosed heart failure patient, the nurse would assess for shortness of breath, fluid retention, and other key signs and symptoms. Understanding and anticipating the particular needs of the patient in relation to the illness is key to the diagnostic role of the nurse.

The **monitoring role** of the nurse is all-encompassing, staying tuned to the individual throughout the hospital stay (or throughout the encounter if in a community encounter). The nurse is present, assessing the individual's interaction with the environment (physical, social, cultural) and keeping the patient safe.

The nurse's **intervention role** speaks to the active implementation of treatments and the monitoring of these for the individual's reactions and for their therapeutic value. These nursing interventions include a wide range of therapeutics: medications, techniques, education, and preparation for therapeutics to be administered by other health professionals (e.g., surgery). In addition to the interventions per se, the nurse also monitors the patient's reactions and responses to the interventions and modifies the therapeutics as needed.

The nurse's **role in outcome assessment** (quality and safety) is key to positive patient outcomes. The nurse is responsible for the assessment of the total environment and the individual's relationship to their environment, their treatment, and their overall health. The nurse has the responsibility of coordinating all care and monitoring the outcomes of that care so that there are positive outcomes. Further the nurse's role in building and maintaining a team approach to care, along with colleagues from other professions, is critical to avoiding errors in care and treatment.

Relationship to Quality and Safety Education for Nurses (QSEN) Competencies

QSEN is a national initiative to improve nursing education and practice in patient-centered care, teamwork, evidence-based practice, quality improvement, safety, and informatics. QSEN competencies in each of these dimensions have been developed. Embedded in each of the competencies are the knowledge, skills, and attitudes to be developed by the nurse (QSEN, 2025). The QSEN foundation is that the patient or designee is the source of control of his/her own health, and the nurse is a full partner in providing compassionate and coordinated care based on respect for the patient's preferences, values, and needs. For each of the six areas identified in the QSEN model, the following objectives have been delineated:

Knowledge

1. Describe how diverse cultural, ethnic, and social backgrounds function as sources of patient, family, and community values.
2. Explore ethical and legal implications of patient-centered care.
3. Discuss principles of effective communication.

Skills

1. Engage patients or designated surrogates in active partnerships that promote health, safety, well-being, and self-care management.
2. Recognize the boundaries of therapeutic relationships.
3. Facilitate informed patient consent for care.

Attitudes

1. Value the patient's expertise with own health and symptoms.

2. Seek learning opportunities with patients who represent all aspects of human diversity.

(QSEN, 2025)

Benner's Model for Nursing Knowledge Development

Theorist Patricia Benner began her journey to discover the knowledge embedded in nursing practice in the early 1980s, representing a scholarly effort to embed nursing theoretical knowledge with the reality of the clinical experience of nurses in professional practice. Prior delineations of nursing knowledge were perceived as distinct from clinical practice and thus not directly applicable. Benner's work, focused on uncovering nursing practice knowledge, was an effort to expand our theoretical understanding of practical knowledge in nursing. The Benner model is a direct application of the Dreyfus (1980) model of skill acquisition to the professional practice of nursing. As with the Dreyfus model, Benner describes that in developing skill acquisition, the nurse passes through the five levels of proficiency: novice, beginner, competent, proficient, and expert. In her theory of clinical nursing practice, Benner (1984) outlined the following dimensions in relation to each of the levels of proficiency.

Novice:

Understands each patient encounter and experience as a new learning.
Focuses on each patient encounter as unique.
Able to apply basic nursing skills.
Needs to develop and integrate learning across clinical encounters.

Advanced beginner:

Builds on prior clinical experiences.
Develops beginning recognition of patterns across clinical situations.
Draws inferences from one clinical encounter to others.

Competent:

Recognizes patterns consistently through analysis across patient situations and encounters.
Able to integrate current clinical experiences with past learning and prior clinical experiences.
Recognizes long-range aspects of own encounters with patients and effects on patients' health.

Proficient:

Able to think holistically.
Learning across patient encounters and clinical situations allows nurses to determine relationships of patterns across clinical encounters and patient experiences
Characterized by learning from experiences.

Expert:

Holistic nursing practice at its highest level.
Focus on the total situation.
Reflective practice.
Able to fully integrate the person, environment, health, and nursing metaparadigm concepts into their clinical practice.
Highest level of emotional intelligence.

Summary of the Benner Model

Each of these stages of knowledge development builds on past learning, with full integration based on prior learning in clinical experiences and skills, and the integration of one's knowledge. Expert nursing practice is the goal for professional nurses and nursing. The expert nurse fully integrates understandings of the holistic nature of persons and their health and intervenes to help the individual move toward a healthier life.

NCLEX-RN Integrated Processes Categories

Licensing regstered nurses into practice is regulated by each of the National Council of State Boards of Nursing (NCSBN). NCSBN adminsters the registered nurse licensing exam, NCLEX-RN and has identified six integrated processs that are fundamental for nursing: caring, clinical judgment, communication and documentation, culture and spirituality, nursing process, and teaching and learning. The authors of this book have aligned narratives to NCSBN's six integrated process and have matched the narratives in each integrated process category to the Benner Model of Knowledge Development.

References

American Nurses Association. (2025). Code of ethics for nurses. American Nurses Publishing. Retrieved May 19, 2025, from https://codeofethics.ana.org/.

Benner, P. (1984). *From novice to expert: Excellence and power in clinical nursing practice.* Menlo Park, CA: Addison-Wesley.

Carper, B. A. (1978). Fundamental patterns of knowing in nursing. *Advances in Nursing Science,* 1: 13–23.

Carper, B. A. (1999). *Fundamental patterns of knowing in nursing. Perspectives on philosophy of science in nursing: An historical and contemporary anthology.* Philadelphia: Lippincott.

Caputi, L. (2021). *Think like a nurse: The Caputi method for learning clinical judgment.* Chicago: Windy City Publishers.

Dreyfus, S. E., & Dreyfus, H. L. (1980). *A five-stage model of the mental activities in directed skill acquisition.* Unpublished report supported by the Air Force Office of Scientific Research. University of California, Berkeley.

Galinas, L. (2025). Updated code of ethics for nurses released: A constant and ready reference. *American Nurse Journal*, 20: 4.

Goleman, D. (2005). *Emotional intelligence: Why it can matter more than IQ.* New York: Bantam Books.

International Council of Nurses. (2025). International council of nurses. Retrieved May 15, 2025, from https://www.icn.ch/

National Council of State Boards of Nursing (n.d.). *NCLEX.* https://www.nclex.com/

Quality and Safety in Nursing (QSEN). (2025). QSEN institute. Retrieved May 15, 2025, from https://www.qsen.org/

Smith, M., & Leihr, P. (2005). Story theory: Advancing nursing practice scholarship. *Holistic Nursing Practice*, 19(6): 272–276. https://doi.org/10.1097/00004650-200511000-00008

World Health Organization. (2025). World Health Organization: Constitution—Definition of health. Retrieved May 15, 2025, from https://www.who.int/about/governance/constitution/

Chapter 2

Caring: Introduction

To care is to be human. Nurses care instinctively because they do what is perhaps the most human-centered act. Nurses consider humanity in every action and every word. To be a successful nurse is to meet patients, families, colleagues, and communities exactly where they are, not where we think they should be, but where they are in the exact moment of the nursing encounter. It is the nurse's duty to consider the entire picture of what led to the moment of the nursing encounter and craft a nurse-driven collaborative plan of care to enhance the future of their patient(s). It is not enough to be well educated or experienced or confident; the nurse must be a caring individual and remember that what may be an objective experience for the nurse may be the worst or best day for their patient(s). The narratives in this chapter highlight exemplary moments of caring that reveal a patient and/or family-centered approach to caring.

The novice story discusses the nurse author's connection between classical music and nursing. This individual's experience as a trained classical musician informs the way she cares for others because it is what shapes her as a human. The story

DOI: 10.4324/9781003586548-2

also mentions the importance of empathy when walking into a patient's room. Lastly, the nurse author highlights how putting oneself in another's shoes, whether it be the patient or family members, strengthens the ability to lead care for others with a caring and thoughtful approach.

The beginner story is a heart-wrenching story of a nurse caring for a patient in the Neonatal Intensive Care Unit. The connection the nurse author created with the mother of the patient during her time in the unit is long-lasting due to the caring approach the nurse forged. To this day, this patient experience informs how the nurse approaches her care for others.

The competent narrative comes from a nurse working in a labor and delivery unit. The narrative showcases the nurse author doing a small gesture that had a major impact. A memento box for the remembrance of a loss showed how much the nurse cares for the patient and family and gave the patient courage to carry on. Eventually, we, the readers, see that this gesture stayed with the patient for years to come.

The proficient narrative is a story about human connection. Connecting with a patient and seeing them "where they are" through finding a common bond is what made this nurse-patient encounter successful. Instead of labeling this patient "impossible," the nurse author found a common bond, the love of dogs, and used the connection to drive a successful and meaningful interaction for the patient and the professional nurse.

Lastly, the expert narrative is a story from the height of the COVID-19 pandemic written by a critical care nurse practitioner. The story is a reminder that our patients are humans too. In the narrative, the nurse author reveals that she needed and appreciated the reminder that her patient in the bed was a patient, a fellow nurse, and a wife. This centered the care she was able to provide with a caring and human focus.

Caring: Novice

Narrative by Jill Cohen, DNP, RN, CNOR, NEA-BC

My journey into nursing was never a straight line. It took a winding path that led me to where I am now, a nurse leader in an operating room. When I was 15, a friend of mine said "let's take a certified nurse assistant (I) class." She knew that there were flexible, well-paying jobs at the nursing home in our hometown. That hometown being in one with a population of 800 people in Northeast Nebraska. So, we started taking a 60 mile journey to our class that summer. Once completing the class, I would have to wait six months until my 16th birthday to take my exam for my I license. The supervisor allowed me to work as an environmental aid in the interim. The nursing home had never had an environmental aide, so I was creating the job responsibilities from scratch. This was the first time that I started to think about how nurses and nurses' aides impact patients. It was also a unique group of people, as these patients were residents of my hometown and individuals that I had grown up interacting with. What could I do in that four hours that would make a difference? I started out refreshing waters. But where I found my purpose was in a simple task; helping the patients put on their sweaters. This gave me the time to connect with each person as well as prepare them for their mealtime. Knowing that the work I did had value made a real impression on me. That impression was so deep seated that it took years of other experiences for me to remember that it was still there.

After high school I spent the next several years doing anything but nursing. When I was sure that my classical music career, a career that I had enjoyed for seven years, wasn't what I wanted to do for the rest of my life, I started to consider other careers. Nursing kept coming to the forefront of those thoughts. I hadn't been inside of any type of medical facility for over seven years, and I was sure a lot had changed. I retested for my I license and got a job at a rehabilitation hospital. That job was difficult. I was working on the spinal cord care unit, and it was heavy, exhausting work. The patients were young men and women who had gone through some type of traumatic event. They never expected to be in the position they were. These patients were so easy to connect with. They were the same people you saw at pool parties, driving home from their first job, or playing team sports with. The mental fortitude to sit in that traumatic space with them required a part of me that I didn't know I had. While I had experienced death in my hometown nursing home, those deaths were likely expected. These patients weren't dying but figuring out how to live again in a much different way. I still remember my first day when the chief nursing officer stood up and said, "you're going to be meeting people on what is likely the worst day of their life. No one comes into this hospital because they chose to." Those powerful words still sit with me. In the busyness of the day, I am often drawn back to her words and recenter before approaching a patient.

I wasn't surprised by how much I connected with the nursing profession, but I was surprised by how much it fulfilled me. Classical music fulfilled me in a way that allowed for my creative side to come through, but that creativity still existed within my nursing career. Along with still maintaining my creativity, I was happy to be part of a team. Classical musicians spend many long, lonely hours by themselves in the practice room. They are also focused on competition. I found nursing to be the opposite. Everyone was focused on teamwork. There's not a shift that anyone can get through without a team. Some of my best childhood memories were being part of teams. I grew up in a small town and played every sport that was offered, mainly because if I wasn't playing that sport, we probably weren't going to have enough people for a team. It was during those times of sitting through long track meets or going to softball tournaments that you connected with people on a different level. I found those same connections in the hospital. I found really great people that I was connecting with not only at the hospital, but also becoming friends outside of the hospital.

During an interview for a Nursing position early in my career, the hiring manager said to me, "can you tell us why you think classical music would help you as a nurse?" I was able to explain how I was used to working with a large group of people, being aware of the other people around you, paying attention to detail, naturally using your creative brain, etc. At the end of the interview, she said she still didn't see how it applied. Those words hurt. I felt that all my life journeys made me a better nurse. It didn't matter whether the experiences I had were in the hospital or in classical music; I was learning how to be a compassionate person, a reflective person, a proactive person, and someone who worked to understand the entire process of anything I was doing. Now I am the person who is hiring new nurses, and whenever I see a résumé of an applicant who came to the profession as a second career, I immediately interview them. These are the nurses that bring a wealth of experience to the hospital and are successful. I have yet to hire a second career nurse who has not excelled at their job.

Nursing is not easy. There are two specific instances that still weigh on me to this day. These experiences were hard to live through and fundamentally changed me. I had two patients "fire me." These patients said that I wasn't doing my job or that my personality or my approach was wrong. It was during this time that I began to realize how self-reflective nurses must be. When I think back to the first patient, I realize that I walked into her room with an approach that wasn't empathetic. I didn't "read the room." I lost sight of the idea that this was the worst day of her life because I, myself, was having a great day. While some could view this as a simple error, it was impactful in a negative way on that patient. As a nurse leader, self-reflection is woven into our standard work, but those reflection skills start at the bedside. If I had walked out on the days I was "fired" and reflected, I don't think I would be enjoying a successful nursing career.

I can now say that I have eventually found the niche part of nursing that connects with me on a deeper level – perioperative nursing. I started as an endoscopy nurse and being in the procedure room was one of the most exciting things that I've ever done. I loved the hustle and bustle of the day, and I also loved that the day came to an end. We could wrap it up in a pretty bow. We could tell everyone how many patients we had cared for, and then at the end of the day, all those patients were either in their inpatient hospital beds or at home. I've now been a leader in almost every area of the perioperative nursing department. As I think about what the next steps will be for me, I will be wholly satisfied to be a perioperative nurse for the rest of my career. Finding that connection in nursing is part of what brings me job satisfaction. The connection with your colleagues is another vital part of job satisfaction. My nursing team has changed as I moved from the bedside to leadership. That team is just as important now as it was when I was bedside. I can't say that every day is fun, but every day has fun moments. We all go through tough days and have to make tough decisions. Sometimes these decisions are life-altering. When I think about nursing, I always tell everyone that it's a human job. Nurses always think about the whole patient. That means we will be part of the highest highs and the lowest lows. I'm honored that our patients trust us with providing care for their whole selves. It's something that I will never take likely and continue to strive to improve.

Reflecting back to my earlier days in Nursing on the spinal cord unit at the rehabilitation hospital, I was assigned to care for one of my colleagues. After receiving the influenza vaccination, one of the nurses in our hospital developed

Guillaume-Barre. Someone who just weeks ago was helping me lift and turn patients was now one of my patients requiring that same heavy care. What struck me was how non-despondent this nurse was. The nurse was not devastated by this illness but rather approached it from a place I would have never gone. They knew that there was a small chance of developing this illness by taking the influenza vaccine, but ultimately the benefit outweighed the risk. There was an unspoken optimism in their approach to each day. It was as if the nurse knew they were going to get better. This is not to say that the therapy involved did not test this nurse each day, but it was as if the nurse knew that it was all worth it. As if they knew the outcome before it was evident to the rest of us. To this point in my career, I had never personally encountered the idea that modern medicine could be harmful. In my current role, this is something that is grappled with daily. As we urgently brought a dissecting aortic aneurysm to the operating room the other day, I once again came face-to-face with the fact that while medicine can heal, in this case, this patient was likely going to die in the OR or the ICU. For the family that made the decision to send their loved one to surgery, they had to weigh the same risk versus benefit scenario that the nurse taking that influenza vaccine had to make all those years ago. While the scenarios have different complexities, it speaks to the gray areas that confound patients and medical professionals.

Another one of the first patients I met was a young man who came from the same area as me. This teenager seemed like your typical Midwest high schooler who excelled in everything he did. One of the things he excelled in was playing football. During the semi-final game of the conference championship, he went for what looked like to everyone, a clean tackle. What happened next was unfathomable. This athlete never got up. He had a high cervical break that would lead him to be paralyzed, except for his fingers, wrists, and a little bit of elbow movement. Walking into his room I was greeted with a family that looked so much like mine. We knew similar people and frequented the same places. My heart broke for them, but I knew the worst thing I could do was pity them. There was no place for pity on the spinal cord unit. Where I knew I could form a connection was in their commitment to working hard. Coming from Nebraska, hard work is instilled in every rural community. So together we all worked hard. I patiently waited and prompted as he tried to transfer from the bed to the wheelchair or as his parents attempted to learn a new skill, such as catheterization. While I could have saved time doing these tasks for them, I wasn't going home with them. We all knew if we worked hard, he was going to be as independent as possible. While the therapists did the bulk of this work, I found that reinforcing what was learned in every encounter I had with him was the best thing I could do for this family.

Reflection

This narrative highlights so many crucial aspects important to the field of nursing. The narrative begins with the author highlighting the importance of teamwork and how the smallest of tasks were paramount in the eyes of her colleagues, patients, and families. The author also highlights how the intersectionality of so many fields with nursing, even music, can enrich your career. If you are a second-degree nursing student or professional, you can draw upon the experiences you have in your non-nursing fields. We start and end each day as humans, and our life and educational experiences enrich our ability to help others. The author's work as a Certified Nurse Assistant prepared her for the field of compassionate nursing. Those phrases heard early in her career still ring true: "meeting patients on their worst days of their lives." The author never lost perspective. The first reflection here may be to never lose sight of your why. Why did you choose to pursue the discipline of nursing? What will be the phrase you tell yourself as you enter each day of your work to ensure you are the grounded and compassionate human you would want taking care of you?

The second takeaway for this narrative may be about her first patient she took care of, the football spinal cord injury patient. What did she ensure not to do when taking care of him and the family? She was compassionate, of course, but shared she never showed the feeling of pity for the patient and family. Why not? This can highlight the caring philosophy we have as nurses and how the feeling of hopelessness is transferable and that we, as nurses, have the privilege to empower those we care for through our words and actions. A sample question:

The nurse walks into a patient room after meeting with the neurosurgical team and notices the patient crying with. After sitting at the bedside with the patient, which of the following responses by the Nurse is best?

- **"What did the team just tell you to make you feel this way?"**
- **"I understand how you feel and I would be upset with this news too."**
- **"Which part of this is making you the most upset right now?"**
- **"I'm going to sit here and we can process this together."**

The first response shows that you are not engaging with the medical teams prior to entering the patient room, which is part of best practice. Nurses and interprofessional team members must be united and in constant communication about plans of care, and asking the patient to relay what the team just communicated can cause a loss of trust in the teamwork that is necessary in safe and highly reliable patient care.

Sharing with the patient that you understand how they feel shows a sense of empathy, but isn't being truthful. You, as the nurse, don't understand (hopefully that is) how it feels to be in the patient's position with a devastating spinal cord injury. Telling the patient in a time of emotional crisis that you understand how they feel can be degrading and dismissive of the patient's feelings.

Asking the patient what part of this is most upsetting isn't allowing the patient time to grieve and process.

While all the above responses may be typical reactions you might have, the most therapeutic and caring response would be the last option, showing that you, as the nurse, are there for the patient and allowing time to process the news the clinical team just shared.

Caring Narrative: Beginner

Narrative by Gloria Gomez, MSN, RN, FNP, NE-BC

At the time of writing this narrative, I am a Doctor of Nursing Practice (DNP) student with a background as a nurse leader. Over the years, I have held various roles in nursing, from bedside care to administrative positions, which have shaped my perspective on leadership and professionalism in healthcare. Currently, I serve as a Registered Nurse in Occupational health, where I focus on employee health and safety.

Leadership in nursing is the ability to guide and inspire others to achieve common goals while fostering an environment of trust, collaboration, and continuous learning. Leadership in nursing is a dynamic and multifaceted role that goes beyond simply managing tasks or directing others. At its core, leadership is about inspiring and empowering those around you to achieve both individual and collective goals. A strong nurse leader must possess a clear vision and be able to articulate that vision in a way that motivates the team by fostering a shared sense of purpose. Leadership also involves being adaptable and responsive to the ever-changing demands of healthcare, making informed decisions in high-pressure situations, and taking responsibility for those decisions. Moreover, leadership requires emotional intelligence – the ability to understand and manage one's own emotions, as well as the emotions of others. This skill is crucial for building strong relationships, resolving conflicts, and maintaining a positive work environment. A true nurse leader is also a mentor, guiding less experienced colleagues in their professional development and helping them navigate the complexities of the nursing profession. By setting an example of integrity, empathy, and excellence, a nurse leader influences the culture of the workplace, contributing to better patient outcomes and a more cohesive, motivated team.

Professionalism in nursing encompasses a broad range of behaviors and attitudes that reflect a commitment to ethical principles, quality care, and continuous self-improvement. It involves consistently demonstrating respect for patients, colleagues, and the profession itself. Professionalism means upholding the standards of practice and adhering to the ethical codes established by nursing bodies, such as maintaining patient confidentiality, providing care without bias, and advocating for the patient's best interests.

In practice, professionalism is evident in how a nurse presents themselves, communicates, and handles challenging situations. This includes being punctual, reliable, and maintaining a calm and composed demeanor, even under stress. It also means being accountable for one's actions and decisions, recognizing the importance of lifelong learning, and seeking out opportunities for professional growth. Another critical aspect of professionalism is collaboration. In a multidisciplinary healthcare environment, nurses must work effectively with other professionals, valuing their expertise, and contributing their own unique insights to achieve the best possible outcomes for patients. Professionalism also requires cultural competence – the ability to provide care that is respectful of and responsive to the cultural and spiritual needs of patients.

In summary, leadership and professionalism in nursing are intertwined concepts that are essential for delivering high-quality care and fostering a positive, supportive work environment. Leadership is about guiding and inspiring others, while professionalism is about embodying the values and standards of the nursing profession in every aspect of one's practice. Together, these qualities ensure that nurses are not only effective caregivers but also respected and influential members of the healthcare team.

One of the most profound experiences of my nursing career involved the care of a young pediatric oncology patient working in the Pediatric Intensive Care Unit (PICU). She was a vibrant, twelve-year-old girl diagnosed with stage four neuroblastoma. Her journey was a difficult one, filled with cycles of hope and despair, as she underwent numerous rounds of chemotherapy, radiation, and experimental treatments. Despite the severity of her condition, she maintained a remarkable spirit, often drawing pictures for the nursing staff and comforting her mother with wisdom far beyond her years.

As her primary nurse, I was deeply involved in her care, from managing her pain and symptoms to providing emotional support to her and her family. One night she needed to be placed on dialysis. During that time only the fellows had been trained on setting up the CVVH machine. It was a busy night with a trauma case coming in and there was one fellow overnight who said she was too busy and if she needed to be placed on dialysis that I had to do it. As a new graduate nurse in the PICU, it was an overwhelming feeling of despair and fear. I knew that her vital signs would not improve if dialysis was not started. Her mother was also urging the team to move the process along. My friend was on the same shift with me and when she heard what was going on she held my hand and said Gloria we got this and we will do this together. We worked together, my friend reading the instructions and I set up the machine. The moment of truth came and it was time to connect her to the dialysis machine and start treatment. I prayed the entire time to all the saints in the heavens that everything would work and help her. To my relief, and that of my friend it did. Her blood pressure normalized and her breathing improved.

Over time, I developed a close bond with her and her mother, sharing in their fears, hopes, and the overwhelming uncertainty that surrounded her condition. Despite all efforts, it became increasingly clear that her disease was not responding to treatment. The PICU team, consisting of compassionate and skilled physicians, delivered the heartbreaking news to her mother: there were no more curative options left.

Faced with this reality, I found myself in the position of not only continuing to care for her physical needs but also helping her mother navigate the complex and painful process of letting go. This period required a delicate balance of providing honest information while also offering comfort and support. I coordinated with the palliative care team to ensure that her pain was well managed and that her remaining time was as peaceful and comfortable as possible.

One of the most challenging moments came when her mother, exhausted and grief-stricken, asked me how she could possibly say goodbye to their daughter. As a nurse, I was trained to provide care and support, but this was a situation that tested every aspect of my professionalism and humanity. I listened to her fears and sorrow, allowing her to express her pain without interruption. I offered gentle guidance, suggesting she focused on sharing her love with her daughter, creating lasting memories, and ensuring she felt surrounded by her care.

In her final days, her condition deteriorated rapidly. She was mostly unresponsive, but I continued to talk to her, reassuring her that she was not alone. I stayed with her through the night, holding her hand and ensuring she was comfortable. She passed away peacefully in the early hours of the morning, with her mothers by her side. This experience shaped me in many ways. After she passed away, I made a promise that if I had a daughter, I would name her the same name as this remarkable patient to remind me of the remarkable young lady that I had the opportunity to meet. Five years after her passing I was blessed with a beautiful little girl, who of course I named the same name.

Caring for her was a deeply emotional and transformative experience that taught me invaluable lessons about the essence of nursing, leadership, and professionalism. One of the most significant lessons I learned is the power of simply being present. In situations where there are no more medical interventions left to offer, the role of the nurse shifts from being a caregiver to a companion in the patient's final journey. Providing comfort, listening, and offering a reassuring presence can be as important as any clinical intervention. This experience highlighted the ethical complexities involved in end-of-life care, particularly in pediatrics. It reinforced the importance of respecting the wishes of the patient and their family while also providing them with the necessary information to make informed decisions. Balancing honesty with empathy is crucial, as is recognizing when to step back and allow the family space to grieve.

Finally, this experience taught me about the need for resilience in nursing. Caring for a dying child is emotionally draining and can lead to feelings of helplessness and burnout. It is crucial for nurses to seek support, whether through peer debriefing, counseling, or self-care practices, to process these experiences and continue to provide compassionate care without compromising their own well-being.

For nurses working in any area where end-of-life care is a reality, it is important to remember that while you may not be able to change the outcome, you can profoundly impact the patient and their family's experience during their final days. Maintain open, honest, and compassionate communication with the patient and their family. Ensure that they understand their options and feel supported in making decisions that are best for them. Never underestimate the importance of your presence. Sometimes, the most meaningful support you can offer is simply being there, providing comfort through your presence and touch. Embrace open communication and be willing to challenge the status quo when it doesn't serve the patient's best interests. Leadership is not just about making decisions; it's about guiding others to make the best decisions together.

Reflection

This author has many reflections on how leadership and nursing are intertwined. No matter the formal titles you may have throughout your career in nursing, we must always remember that we are leaders. We lead the care for our patients and collaborate with our interprofessional team members throughout the continuum. We, as nurses, are in the most trusted profession and therefore must act as such. We have the responsibility to be role models for those within and those external to the healthcare arena, and we must always hold ourselves and each other to a high standard of excellence.

This author's narrative also tells the heartbreaking and perhaps heartwarming story of one young patient. This author's narrative highlights the humanity necessary in our field – the crucial caring component that we must always remember. We see patients and families as they are and meet them where they need us most. The author highlights a moment of advocacy and teamwork when setting up the dialysis machine to ensure the patient receives the best care when needed most. Moments like this happen often in our discipline…when we must rely on our knowledge, resourcefulness, and teamwork to get a task done when it may seem impossible. This narrative also reveals a moment in time when they needed to advocate for the patient's family to be present and be aware of the impending death of their beloved daughter. Through the author's caring actions and words, the author helped the family cope and accept the loss, and therefore allowed the patient's family to grieve in real time and process a tragic occurrence. A sample question surrounding this narrative:

The nurse learns of a patient's decline and understands that death is imminent in their shift. The patient's family remains at the bedside and has been informed by the interprofessional team. The best course of action would for the Nurse be to:

- **Give the family private and alone time and avoid going to the patient's room, knowing that nothing can be done.**
- **Call psychiatric services as a consult to help the family during this time.**
- **Go to the patient's room immediately and allow the patient's family to verbalize their feelings while inquiring if they would like to be visited by pastoral services/chaplaincy or social services.**
- **Review the patient's medical record and determine what religion the family may be, and ask for a chaplain immediately**

The best course of action is to go to the patient's room and listen, and then inquire and assess what the patient's family's preferences and needs are. The first response is avoidance and does not offer a therapeutic and caring approach. The second and fourth options are assumptive and do not take the patient's family's preferences into consideration.

Caring Narrative: Competent

Narrative by Ashley Kovacs, MSN, RNC-OB, C-EFM

With over 20 years of experience in labor and delivery nursing, I have dedicated my career to supporting women and families during some of the most life-changing moments. I began my journey as a Licensed Vocational nurse (LVN), eventually advancing to an RN II in labor and delivery. My path also led me to Dallas, where I honed my clinical and leadership skills. Later, I served as a charge nurse in labor and delivery as well as an ANM, overseeing patient care and guiding my team through both routine and extraordinary situations. Most recently, I worked as an Ambulatory Team Lead in a women's health clinic, where I continue to grow as a leader while improving care delivery.

To me, leadership is about more than managing tasks – it's about creating a supportive environment where both patients and staff feel valued. It means stepping in when needed, showing empathy, and ensuring that every individual under my care is treated with dignity and compassion. Three years ago, while working as a charge nurse in labor and delivery, I had an experience that reminded me of the profound impact we can have as nurses, not just in the moment, but for years to come.

I cared for a patient during one of the hardest moments of her life: the loss of her baby. As her labor and delivery nurse, I knew my role extended far beyond clinical tasks. I stayed by her side, offering emotional support and ensuring she had the space to grieve. To honor her baby's memory, I created a personalized memento box that I hand drew a picture on. It included a lock of hair, tiny handprints and footprints, a handwritten note of encouragement from the nurses on staff that night, and a small candle for remembrance. She clung to that box, telling me it gave her something tangible to hold on to during her darkest days.

Fast forward to the next year. I was the charge nurse on a busy labor and delivery shift. One of my nurses asked me to help her clean up a patient who had just delivered and prepare her for transfer to the postpartum floor. I stepped into the room and introduced myself to the patient. Before I could say anything else, her eyes met mine, and she gasped. "It's you," she said softly. "You were with me last year when I lost my first baby." Her voice trembled as she continued. "That memory box you made for me…it meant everything. I still have it. It helped me heal and gave me the strength to hope for this moment."

I looked over to the beautiful, healthy baby asleep in the bassinet in the corner, and tears welled up in my eyes. The patient shared how the care and compassion she received during her loss made her feel supported and understood. She wanted me to know the impact I had made on her journey. As I stood there, helping my nurse and the patient transition to this new chapter, I was reminded why I became a nurse. While clinical excellence is essential, the human connection – the ability to offer comfort and compassion during life's most profound moments – is what truly defines the heart of nursing.

My advice is to remember that compassionate care is at the heart of our profession. Patients may not always recall the clinical tasks you performed, but they will never forget how you made them feel. Stay curious and open to learning – every experience is an opportunity to grow. Seek out mentors, ask questions, and embrace the wisdom of your colleagues. Take time to reflect on your experiences, both positive and challenging, as this will help you grow and refine your practice. Most importantly, stay resilient. There will be tough moments, but holding on to your purpose and celebrating small victories will remind you why you chose this incredible journey.

Reflection

This author writes about the importance of remembering the human aspect of the discipline of nursing and how the seemingly inconsequential actions we take in our roles can have the biggest impact. This narrative highlights a human action of creating a memento or memory box for the loss of a patient and its role in grieving and processing death. This story hopefully urges the readers to be curious about the resources and options at their place of work. Do you know about your ethics committee, any death protocols, any pastoral or chaplaincy referrals you can make, and any other practices and offerings available at your institution? If not, pause, and possibly do some research so you are most empowered should a time come when you need to offer something beyond yourself to your patients and families.

A potential question related to this narrative is:

The nurse cares for a clinically stable labor and delivery patient after a stillbirth. The nurse's spouse is at the bedside and is requesting for their eight-year-old child to visit. The nurse understands the best response is:

- **"Unfortunately, young children under the age of thirteen are not able to visit, but once you are transferred to the postpartum floor, they may visit."**
- **"Yes however, may I ask if they understand what has happened and may I offer assistance in any way in communicating?"**
- **"Of course they may visit during this time."**
- **"No unfortunately, but we can arrange a video conference call."**

The first response may be dismissive of the patient's and spouse's request to be united as a family. While the visitation guideline is typical for adult critical care areas to limit visitation for minors, visitation guidelines are only guidelines and exceptions can always be made, especially for a clinically stable patient during a time of need. The third response does not consider the possible need for education for the patient, spouse, and young child. Visiting a labor and delivery unit in a hospital may be overwhelming, especially considering the stillbirth. The fourth response does not offer a caring and therapeutic approach, and while the nurse is offering a possible compromise, a video conference in this circumstance may not be sufficient. The best response is the second due to the nurse offering an exception to the possible visitation guidelines while also offering caring education to ensure the patient and family are well prepared to understand the next steps. This conversation can be a segue into understanding what the patient and the family as a unit need to cope with and process the loss of the baby.

Caring Narrative: Proficient

Narrative by Mallory Potondi, BSN, RN, CCRN, SRNA

Being a leader to me means that no matter what has been told to you by coworkers about a patient, you treat them with dignity and respect. Patients are at the hospital against wanting to be there, and often isolated, away from friends, family, and any sense of comfort that they have at home. If a unit full of my coworkers couldn't stand a patient, I always tried to go in with a new mindset and not let other nurses' feelings change the way I approached meeting a new patient.

I can't begin to count how many times I've performed CPR, and I can't begin to count how many times I've put a body into a bag. I can't begin to count how many times I've walked into the unit to be told the patient I took care of the previous shift died overnight. I can't even count the number of times myself or a coworker was assigned three patients instead of one because we were short-staffed, or how many lunch breaks we missed.

I also can't guess how many times after a traumatic experience or patient death, I turned around to act like nothing happened because the patient in the next room was ready to be discharged, needed a glass of water, or needed their next infusion. I can tell you – that you become detached and numb to all the above. It's easy for something that once felt like a life-changing trauma to become another mundane task when you live through it as a part of your day-to-day job. It becomes easy to forget the patients we're caring for and their families are not immune and numb to the trauma and death that is second nature to us.

In the heart failure and cardiac ICU in which I was a nurse, I acted as a charge nurse, a preceptor, helped with students, and participated in committees run by our shared governance on the unit. I always felt teamwork was essential to being an unspoken leader, and that being a team player would encourage those around me to find their strengths and embrace them as skills essential for the needs of our unit.

Some patients stop you in your tracks and take you by surprise, without even knowing it. There was a patient who was said to be "kind of a grumpy guy and difficult to take care of at times," which always seemed to be the type of patient that I ended up getting along with. So, I wasn't nervous about the shift ahead of me. I became the type of nurse on our unit who was looked to as a leader, someone who could handle the "difficult personalities" with patience and care.

This particular patient had four dogs at home while he was sent urgently to us for advanced heart failure exacerbation and planning for left ventricular assistive device (LVAD) implantation. His wife said they were confused about why he wasn't home and eager to see him. This was how I connected with them I'm a dog lover, and instantly we understood each other. He was indeed a "grumpy guy," but I was able to banter back at him, and he would get a kick out of it. I wanted this guy to know that I was on his side, so I searched YouTube for a video on how to make a towel animal, the kind you see in hotels waiting to greet you on the bed. I made him a towel dog. I wasn't going to be back at work for several days and I wanted him to know that I would be thinking of him and wanted him to have something in the dark and gloomy hospital room that brought happiness to him. He loved his towel dog.

I got back the next week from my long stretch of days off. I was listening to all the stories about the patients over the time I was away. Everyone kept talking about the "terrible code," but I wasn't really catching much of the story until several hours later. It was my buddy, he died, and I was so sad.

I found peace in the fact that I was able to see him and treat him as an individual and make my own assessment of this patient without forming an opinion based on every nurse before me. Sure, I always listened to the report I was given, took into consideration what a coworker would say to me, but I always began the patient-nurse relationship with a fresh perspective, no matter what I was told by the previous nurse. I was happy that. I got to know him and care for him in a way that wasn't tarnished by previous opinions of how he was "so grumpy and difficult." I genuinely enjoyed taking care of him for several shifts and getting to know him and his wife. Had I not made an attempt to form my own opinion, his experience, in what I didn't know would be his final days, could have been much different. I'm thankful for those final days and how he reminded me to always approach patients with this mindset.

Reflection

This narrative once again highlights the importance of staying centered and remembering why one becomes a nurse. The author mentions that the tasks can become mundane and that we may go through our shifts or work and lose focus on what we are actually doing. As nurses, we are healing others, saving lives, advocating, and leading care. While much of the work can seem routine day in and day out, we must always remember the privilege and power we have as leaders at the bedside. The author mentions a "difficult" patient and how, by seeing the patient through a human lens, they were able to form a bond and connect. The reader may be reflecting on their own experiences with those "difficult" patients, but are we asking ourselves – what does this patient need? Would we also be labeled as "difficult" if we were separated from those creature comforts that we have outside the walls of a hospital room? Imagine being isolated from your loved ones, pets, bed, shower, and independence...that is exactly what this narrative's author did when they made a dog out of hospital towels.

Something small once again becoming something so big for a patient. This caring initiative revealed a human bond between the nurse and patient and family and allowed for trust to continue and care to flourish. We must always "see and meet the patient where they are" to have a greater impact.

A sample question related to this narrative may be:

The nurse cares for a delirious 84-year-old patient who is screaming and throwing things. The patient has also recently pulled out their IV and has no IV access. The nurse should take which action next:

- **Call the patient's spouse to reorient the patient and help explain that the nurse will need to place another IV and that the spouse will be back to visit in the morning.**
- **Call the medical team and ask for an order for restraints so the nurse can place an IV.**
- **Wait for the patient to calm down and return to the patient's room when they are settled down.**
- **Turn the TV on for a diversion while you begin cleaning up the room and preparing for the IV insertion.**

While the nurse should understand that delirium is a potential regular occurrence for older adults during a hospital stay, the nurse understands that they need to prioritize IV access to ensure patient safety. Restraints should only be used when all other attempts have been made to keep a patient safe in a hospital. Restraining a patient should be a last resort and is therefore not the best answer in this case because the nurse has not tried to reorient the patient. Avoiding the patient and waiting for the patient to settle down is not appropriate and could potentially allow the situation to escalate. Delirious patients are more likely to fall or cause harm; therefore, the nurse should not leave the bedside at this time. Using diversionary activities such as television or music can de-escalate situations, but without trying to reorient the patient, the nurse is avoiding the cause of delirium and/or allowing the delirious episode to continue without assessment and prioritization of IV access. Contacting the patient's spouse considers the human need of the patient and can potentially assist in de-escalation, allowing the nurse to gain IV access to keep the patient safe. Considering the patient is away from their loved one while in the hospital displays the caring attribute necessary for all nurse-patient relationships.

Caring Narrative: Expert

Narrative by Dorothy Chan, DNP, FNP-C, NPD-BC, CCRN, CNE, CNEcl.

I am a professional development educator. I have worked in areas included telemetry, intermediate care, and emergency medicine. Working during the COVID-19 pandemic was a challenge in many ways. It was a time that challenged our resilience as nurses, and with that came the naked truth as we pushed passed boundaries and mental barriers that held us back. During this time, I worked as a nurse practitioner.

I remember the daily messages asking if I was able to work and cover with the hospitalist, as there were a large number of patients admitted with complications with COVID-19. It was our job to see each patient and assess them on a daily basis. I was frightened and unsure. What if I got my family sick? What if this is the day I saw a patient and wasn't careful in my infection prevention process and got sick? Should I call out and take care of my mental health? Anxious thoughts plagued me on a daily basis.

I remember one particular shift. I looked down at my list of patients, name after name after name. This particular patient I went to see was about halfway down on my list. I remember stopping at the threshold of the room by the closed door. I robotically donned my personal protective equipment, checked my CAPR (Controlled Air Purifying Respirator) helmet. I walked into the room and my eyes looked at the patient in the bed. She was confused, her hair frazzled and unkept by her constant movement. Her eyes darted around the room as she restlessly moved around. I could hear my heart beating in my ears as I walked closer to her, taking one breath at a time. I kept breathing. In and out. In and out. I finally stopped as I reach the bedside. It was only a few steps but it felt like a lifetime, knowing that I was stepping into a space here I could become stricken with COVID-19 if I wasn't careful.

I introduced myself and went to assess her heart and lungs with my disposable stethoscope, the cold, uncomfortable earpieces pushing awkwardly in my ears. Out of the corner of my eyes, I see movement on the lit screen of an IPAD, showing a FaceTime call in progress. I let the person on the other line know I am there and ask who they are.

"Oh, hello. I'm so glad you're there. I'm her husband." I smile and continue my assessment. He asks who I am again. "I'm the nurse practitioner. I'm here to see how your wife is doing today." There was a slight pause. "Please take care of her. I just want her to get better. You know, she's a nurse practitioner too. She's just like you. Please, please take care of her. I can't be there with her but tell her how much I love and miss her."

In that moment, I felt the weight of everything. The physical stress, the mental toll, the emotional drain. I felt his desperation through the call as well as the love he had for his wife. I felt like an imposter. At this time, I didn't feel like a hero; I just felt like I was trying not to drown. But that's not what he needed. His words echoed in my head. "She's just like you." I felt a connection to the patient in the bed. She was probably seeing patients too, like I was doing in that very moment. She studied hard, took the necessary exams, got her license. Just like me. I paused. "Of course, I will take care of her."

I look back at that time now and see the depths of human resilience. We came back day after day and took care of those who needed it. We were vulnerable and unsure, but we overcame in order to continue to do our duty. We stepped up and pulled strength from within ourselves. We were truly heroes at that time. I use this experience to remember that even when we struggle, we can be strong and overcome the challenges we face.

Reflection

This narrative reveals that we never know our patients until we ask. We may see a patient in the bed or a diagnosis in the electronic medical record, but do we always consider the human behind the diagnosis, or the career or family life the patient has or had before they enter the care setting in which we provide care? The author provided care for another nurse, but would the author have known this had the FaceTime call not been in progress when she entered the patient's room? It did not make a difference in the care the patient received, knowing that the patient was a fellow nurse, but it certainly provided context and weight to the situation and the responsibility the author has as a nurse. A potential question prompting us to consider this topic:

The nurse enters a patient room at the beginning of their shift to perform their routine environmental and head-to-toe assessments. After introducing themselves to the patient as their primary nurse, which statement is the most appropriate?

- **"I'm here to perform my assessments. After them, you can ask me any questions you want and we can make a plan."**
- **"I'm here to perform my assessments. I'll tell you what I'm doing but please feel free to ask any questions during and after. I'd also love to know more about you and how we can make your stay as smooth as possible."**
- **"I'm here to perform my assessments. The assessments will tell me where we need to prioritize care and I'll relay my findings to the medical team."**

- **"I'm here to perform my assessments. Stop me when you want but I need to be quick to get the day going."**

All statements explain to the patient that the nurse is there to perform assessments, which is good practice to explain what you are doing at all times. "Narrating care" is a best practice. Telling the patient to ask questions after the assessments are complete does not convey a caring and human aspect, as patients (and families) may want to know what the nurse is doing in real time. While assessments are a crucial aspect of nursing care, they are not the only consideration when understanding what the priorities should be for patients and families; therefore, the third response is not the most appropriate. The last statement foregoes a human and caring milieu and dictates to the patient that they need to stop the nurse if necessary. The last statement also reveals to the patient that the nurse does not consider this time with the patient as a priority. The most appropriate statement is the second option, as it offers a chance for bi-directional sharing. Also, the second option is the only option that reveals to the patient that the human aspect of their needs and background is equally as important as the clinical presentation.

Chapter 3

Clinical Judgment: Introduction

Clinical judgment rooted in critical thinking is a core competency for the professional nurse. The ability to make swift and sound decisions is essential if the nurse is to succeed in the discipline. Critical thinking and developing expert-level clinical judgment are lifelong aspirations that begin in nursing schools. Whether through live or simulated experiences, the student nurse begins to develop clinical judgment. Through a career in nursing, lived experiences are what inform successful clinical judgment. Patients, families, communities, and colleagues rely on nurses for their clinical judgment rooted in experienced lessons of successful patient care. Often, the nurse will be driving the interprofessional collaborative plan of care based on clinical judgment, as the nurse may have the most expert knowledge and years of experience. We nurses lead care through clinical judgment.

The novice nurse reflects on a moment when "listening to her gut" informed her of an impending rapid response for one of her patients. While the care team was ultimately unable to

DOI: 10.4324/9781003586548-3

save the patient's life, the clinical judgment this nurse experienced was a lesson she will always remember.

The beginner nurse recounts a story from an early time in her career when she was new to the charge nurse role. She relied heavily on her clinical judgment to successfully triage the appropriate priority levels of the many patients in the unit.

The competent nurse's story highlights a moment when the primary nurse noticed a clinical change in their patient and immediately escalated the concerning change. When the medical colleague did not notice any concerning clinical change in the patient's status, the nurse continued to escalate their concern based on years of clinical knowledge and clinical judgment. After successfully escalating the clinical concern, the nurse realized that they had potentially saved this patient's life and it all started with an assessment. A worthy and impressive assessment at that.

The proficient nurse author recounts a moment when a patient was disruptive and had the potential to be harmful to himself and to others. The nurse used clinical judgment and decided that offering the patient food and ensuring his blood sugar was addressed was a priority to effectively manage and reduce the patient's blood pressure.

The expert's story reflects on a critical experience that occurred in the operating room. The nurse used clinical judgment and called a cardiac arrest code, which typically is not done due to the protocols that exist in a perioperative setting. The nurse weighed the options and ultimately leaned towards what felt best and most appropriate in the moment.

Clinical Judgment: Novice

Narrative by Kerri Hensler, DNP, MPA, RN, CNOR, NEA-BC

Often when I am asked to share an experience from my professional career, I reflect back to happy moments or moments when I impacted a patient's care for the better. As I learned about the context of this book, I felt that sharing this moment would be more meaningful. The lesson: trust yourself and your gut.

I began my nursing career at a large urban academic medical center, working on a medical step-down unit. The unit was very busy with complex patients, most often coming from the intensive care unit (ICU) as soon as they were clinically appropriate and no longer needed ICU-level care. I was privileged to learn from the most amazing preceptors who exhibited unbelievable clinical knowledge and skill while simultaneously approaching each patient with empathy and grace.

On a particular day, soon after my orientation, I was assigned to three patients, requiring step-down level of care. I received hand off and no alarming concerns were raised. As I began my initial assessment, I could sense that one patient was just…unsettled. Her daughter was at the bedside and shared that the patient (her mom) had been uncomfortable all afternoon. Adding to her discomfort, the patient was attached to continuous monitoring, receiving oxygen through nasal cannula, receiving medication and fluid through her IV, had an indwelling urinary catheter, and was wearing sequential compression devices on her legs to promote blood flow to help prevent blood clots. I reviewed her vital signs, nursing notes, hand-off notes and trends throughout the day, and there was nothing alarming in the clinical presentation that was standing out. As the evening progressed, the patient continued to be uncomfortable and began fidgeting. I was at the bedside often assessing if there was anything changed or was abnormal, but again, nothing stuck out. A little before midnight, I was at the patient's side, and she said to me, "I think I'm going to die." That really alarmed me because she had been unsettled all night, but again, all her vital signs remained stable. I was at a crossroads.

I shared my concerns with the provider and then spoke with my charge nurse and told her that I wanted to call a rapid response because I felt that I was missing something. Together, we called a rapid response team to come help assess this patient. The charge nurse came to the bedside, and we began trying to obtain additional IV access. The rapid response team came to the bedside and assessed the patient. They, too, were unable to find anything that would be causing this patient to be unsettled. As the rapid response team began to walk away, the patient rapidly decompensated and went pulseless. We called a code, and we tried our best to resuscitate her. After over an hour of life-saving efforts, it was determined that we were unable to save this patient. I was devastated.

I remember my patient had blonde hair and was kind. I remember her daughter, who was at the bedside and cared for her day in and day out. I remember she had a gold bracelet on her right hand. I remember she had the corner bed near the window. And I remember the pure shock of the entire team when the patient coded. I was so disappointed in myself that I couldn't figure out what was wrong. That moment will stay with me forever. I learned to trust my gut – even if the vital signs and tests are not revealing the issue. Our job is not to treat the monitor or the numbers but our patients. We spend more time with our patients than anyone else, and if you sense something is wrong and when the patient says they're not OK, our role is to speak up and advocate for them. I hope that my experience will empower you to trust your gut and speak up.

Reflection

This author's narrative showcases treating the patient, not the monitor. When her patient expressed a sense of impending doom, it was a warning sign. The author listened and activated a rapid response, and though it unfortunately wasn't enough to save this patient's life, this nurse should feel confident that they did their best when taking care of this patient. Unfortunately, sometimes the best assessment skills and life-saving efforts aren't enough...but what would this author feel if they had not listened to this patient and had not activated the rapid response team? Do you truly listen to your patients when they tell you something? Because who knows our patients better than themselves and their loved ones? This author escalated the concern and activated an emergency response team because they listened to their gut and relied on their clinical judgment and not solely on the patient's bedside monitor or lab values.

A potential question related to this narrative may be:

An older adult patient is transferred to an orthopedic unit after an open reduction and internal fixation (ORIF) surgery for a tibial fracture. Which scenario below would trigger an emergency response from the patient's nurse:

- **All vital signs are within normal limits except the patient's heart rate is elevated to 110, and the patient expresses extreme hunger and thirst.**
- **All vital signs are within normal limits, but the patient is very groggy and irritable, but able to be re-oriented.**
- **All vital signs are within normal limits except the patient is short of breath, with a respiratory rate of 35, and the patient appears panicked.**

- **All vital signs are within normal limits except the patient's heart rate is 55, and the blood pressure is 98/64.**

The nurse must consider that this is a post-operative patient and is still recovering from anesthesia. The nurse must also consider the pre-operative vital signs and understand this specific patient's baseline for heart rate and blood pressure. Therefore, the last option is not concerning so long as the primary and surgical team are aware of the current vital signs and that the slightly bradycardic heart rate and hypotension are occurring. The first option, with the elevated heart rate and craving for nourishment, could be a human response to not eating for many hours pre-surgery and being hungry. The tachycardic heart rate of 110 could also be a pain response. This clinical presentation needs further assessment, but not an emergency response. The second option is a potential normal post-operative/post-anesthesia presentation. Patients, especially older adults, take longer to recover from anesthesia; therefore, a groggy but re-orientable patient is not concerning and does not warrant an emergency response. However, continuous assessments are necessary to ensure the patient has properly recovered from the procedure and anesthesia. The third option is the most concerning and warrants a potential emergency response. The elevated respiratory rate and panicked presentation could be a warning sign for a pulmonary embolism, which is a complication of orthopedic surgeries.

Clinical Judgment: Beginner

Narrative by Jennifer Ezeokobe, BSN, RN

I was a medical intensive care unit (ICU) nurse for four years in Michigan before moving to Ohio to pursue my doctorate in nurse anesthesia. I was very involved on all the units I worked on, joining projects to help educate nurses on new technological changes, such as teaching the nurses about new electronic medical record charting changes.

Leadership to me is more than just being in charge; it is about guiding others with empathy and clearness. I realize that true leaders don't need to have all the answers themselves, but they do need to be able to create an environment where others feel safe to contribute and collaborate. A great leader listens, helps others grow, and is willing to take a step back to let the team shine when need be. My experiences with leadership have taught me that it's more about service than control. It's being the one who helps others succeed by providing direction, encouragement, and a safe space.

Professionalism on the other hand is how I show up and present myself to the world, especially when things aren't easy. To me, it means maintaining a sense of respect, accountability, and reliability, especially in tough times. It's also about treating others fairly, communicating openly, and following through with things. I believe professionalism also involves staying open-minded, maintaining my integrity, and respecting the integrity of others.

I never really saw myself much of a leader and didn't think I had the qualities to be one until I was kind of forced into it and realized I did have the qualities to be a leader all along. This realization occurred during my first year as a registered nurse in the medical ICU or MICU. I was tasked with being a charge nurse for the night for the first time ever in my career.

I was so afraid to be charge nurse because 1) I was a new nurse 2) I felt like I didn't know enough and therefore couldn't be a good resource for the other nurses on the unit and 3) I had never done it before; granted I did get charge nurse orientation beforehand, but still I was scared.

The night started off pretty smoothly for the first few hours. All the nurses got their tasks done and I was able to help them here and there. I remember thinking, "Being a charge nurse is actually not bad! What was I so worried about?" Boy, was I wrong. That night our unit dealt with a patient who coded two separate times and a difficult patient who tried to leave AMA. Luckily these did not occur at the same time, but I felt like everything that could go wrong went wrong. I started to feel like I jinxed myself. The staff on my unit was so capable and supportive of me and of each other, I truly feel I couldn't have survived that night without them. I was able to support the nurses who had these particular patients. I helped in the code, got the crash cart, and continuously kept checking in on that nurse. I was able to watch and care for that patient while she dealt with her other patients and helped with anything she needed.

As for the difficult patient that tried to leave AMA, I was able to talk with the patient and the patient's family members to hear them out and try to understand why they were acting the way they were. Unfortunately, the patient was not in the right mind, but I still talked with him to see if I could de-escalate things. I also talked with that patient's nurse separately to get her perspective on things. I got security involved to be on standby just in case the patient got violent, and luckily, he never did. Thankfully the doctors are always on unit, so they were aware of everything, but I still kept up with communication with them as well so I could be a part of the planning process for these patients. I made sure that I was supportive of all the staff and tended to their needs. I just wanted to help them anyway I could.

Things cooled finally down, and before I knew it, my first shift as a charge nurse was over. I was so relieved because it was a tough shift for me and the other nurses. That night I ended up learning a lot about myself and how capable I am in tough situations. One nurse even told me I should charge nurse more often. I laughed and thought never again, but I really did appreciate that comment. If there is one thing I can recommend to readers, it is to never doubt yourself. You are more capable than you know. I definitely learned that the hard way. Also, it's okay if you don't know everything and have to rely on others. These qualities can make you a great leader.

Reflection

This author spotlights the importance of leadership and professionalism and to believe in ourselves when taking on a new role, such as a charge nurse role. We may not ever feel ready for a new challenge or role, but with the support of your preceptors, mentors, and a solid team around you, we in nursing are never alone. Don't be afraid to self-identify as ready for a new challenge or role. Ask questions and partner with your passion!

The narrative by this author partly centers around the aspect of a patient leaving against medical advice (AMA). This occurs no matter the setting and at times can be a frenzied experience for the nurse and team. Oftentimes patients are ready for discharge, but due to hospital processes and workflows or human factors, delays may occur for various reasons including, but not limited to, delayed discharge orders, delayed interprofessional rounding, delayed transport, delayed discharge instructions, etc. When delays happen, patients may be frustrated, and let's face it, who wouldn't be frustrated if delayed in leaving the hospital. It is part of the nursing responsibility to keep open lines of communication and set expectations and de-escalate situations as they occur in real time. When caring for an agitated patient, some de-escalation techniques are important. It is crucial to know the patient's history and any underlying diagnoses that may contribute to the potential for violence or aggression. A sample question related to de-escalation may be:

The Charge Nurse is communicating with a patient with a psychiatric diagnosis that may cause agitation and violent behavior. Which of the below may trigger an aggressive or violent response:

- **Explaining that the meal trays are delayed but offering unit-based snacks while waiting.**
- **Communicating that the patient must stay in his room.**
- **Asking if the patient would like to go for a walk.**
- **Obtaining a patient history by asking the patient about their family.**

Offering diversionary activities such as a snack while waiting for a delayed tray is an excellent way to keep the patient occupied and also offers a sense of control by giving them a choice about whether they would like a snack while they wait for their meal tray. Asking the patient if they would like to go for a walk is a health-promoting idea for patients and also offers an opportunity for control. Obtaining a patient history by asking a patient about their family is not only a nursing responsibility, but it also allows for the nurse-patient trusting relationship to form by learning about the patient not only through a clinical lens but through a human lens.

Forming rules and mandating that patients with a psychiatric diagnosis who have the potential for aggression or violence may trigger such acts. Providing patients with control is important. Patients with a psychiatric diagnosis often need socialization and the ability to have control over their schedules. Communicating unit-based expectations in a therapeutic manner while offering patients opportunities to control their schedules reduces the chance of a triggered aggressive response.

Clinical Judgment Narrative: Competent

Narrative by Anonymous

It was about four years into my nursing career and I was working a flexible shift – 1pm–2:30am. I actually liked the alternative hours and it wasn't quite night shift so I didn't have to walk around like a zombie on my days off and totally dread going to work and having to switch my sleep schedule for a few nights per week. It worked for me...for a while...until it didn't. Which is the nice thing about Nursing – there is always another option if something isn't working – right? Well, I digress.

It was about four years into my nursing career and I was working a flexible shift and managing the care of a patient who was recovering from a ventriculoperitoneal (VP) shunt surgery. The patient's vital signs were within normal limits, all outputs were within normal limits, but something suddenly seemed a bit "off" to me. I first recognized this shift when after a few hours with the patient, the patient's behavior and responses to my questions changed. They would answer all my neuro assessment questions correctly and perform my neuro assessment commands appropriately, but it just seemed "off." I immediately called the Neurosurgery resident to the bedside to get their take on the situation and escalate what I was witnessing.

The resident was miffed to be disturbed so late and complained about their case load that evening. As an aside, I do have sympathy for first- and second-year, and frankly all-year residents because yes, they can be overworked. But that is why we are an interprofessional TEAM. We are in place to support each other through trust and collaboration. Also because it was late into the flexible shift, it was in "night crew" territory, meaning there were fewer resources around, adding to the potential feeling of burden when calling in reinforcements. The resident didn't think the change in patient affect was worrisome or clinically relevant and left. I pleaded with them to reconsider, but my nursing voice fell on deaf ears. I went to a few of my colleagues and asked their advice. They said that if I was concerned, listen to my gut feeling. They reminded me that my clinical judgment was based in years of training and schooling, advanced certification, and years of practice and not to be dissuaded by an arrogant and tired team member who didn't agree with me.

I knew the patient's family was down the hall in a family lounge, so I went and asked one of the patient's loved ones to see if they would like to visit the patient for a bit. As soon as the family member entered the room, they said, "umm something is wrong." The spidey sense I had in me was RIGHT! The family member was immediately concerned and said that the patient seemed "not with it" and that they seemed "out of it" and "not like themselves" and "different than when we last saw her a few hours ago." I immediately called the resident back to the bedside while the family member was present so he could hear the historical testimony I was hearing. Once again, the resident didn't seem bothered. He wanted to write it off as just a normal side effect from the surgery and anesthesia. I knew better – this could be a stroke or a failure of the newly created VP shunt. I reassured the family member that I was all over the situation and that we would be escalating this further.

I escalated my concerns to the Neurosurgery Fellow immediately. The Fellow was frustrated I was calling her instead of the resident. When I explained the situation, the Fellow agreed that any small change was worth escalating and thanked me for notifying her. Within fifteen minutes, the Fellow and resident were at the bedside with me. After a more thorough assessment performed by the Fellow, they immediately called the Attending Surgeon and prepared an operating room and the patient for a surgical examination and a possible revision of the VP shunt.

I felt vindicated, but more than that, I felt happy that my clinical judgment, or my "spidey sense," was able to potentially save this fragile patient's life. I was grateful my colleagues empowered me to listen to my clinical judgment. I was honored that a more senior physician partner appreciated my clinical judgment when a junior physician did not. I learned that this experience was a learning and coaching moment for the resident and he later apologized to me. The family member thanked me for being there for the patient and I said, of course – that is what we nurses do. We are here for you.

Reflection

The author of this narrative highlights how important our clinical judgment is! The author saved this patient's life. They could have been satisfied with the simple answers and command responses in their neuro assessments, but when they noticed something was "off," they didn't settle and move on. Instead, the nurse paused and considered what this slight change could potentially mean. This nurse knew that a VP shunt surgery failure was potentially occurring, and the nurse immediately escalated and sought interprofessional collaboration, driving a positive outcome. Bravo!

A potential question related to this scenario is:

Which of the following clinical signs is not a potential sign of increased intracranial pressure?

- **Lethargy**
- **Hypotension**
- **Headache**
- **Vomiting**

Lethargy, headache, and vomiting are all potential signs of increased intracranial pressure. Other signs include, but are not limited to, photosensitivity, pupil size changes, bradycardia, and decreased motor function. Hypotension is not associated with increased intracranial pressure.

Clinical Judgment: Proficient

Narrative by Andriy Melnychenko, BSN, RN, CCRN, TCRN

A couple of years ago, I worked in a medical intensive care unit (MICU). One late afternoon, I received a patient who had missed his dialysis, was in hypertensive emergency, had poor vision, difficulty speaking, and was uncooperative and aggressive. When you hear that in a report, you know the remaining hours of your shift will be hectic. The patient arrived just as described. His systolic blood pressure was 260 mmHg. I attempted to connect the infusion to treat his blood pressure, but the patient was very uncooperative. He was constantly trying to get up, rip his cables off, and pull out his IV. He was also a large man, so it was tough to keep him in bed. My constant reorientation and attempts to prevent him from getting up were not very helpful. His blood pressure was approaching 300 mmHg, and I was worried that he would have a stroke.

At one point, in the middle of everything, I heard him mumble, "Hungry." I tried my best to explain that, at this point, food was not the priority. I told him that he might die if we didn't control his blood pressure. Despite this, he continued to get up and pull on his Ivs. At one point, I thought to myself, if food is what is important to him right now, I will give it to him. Yes, we've all been educated that we have to set boundaries, that we need to prioritize, and that nurses are not there to deliver food. But at that moment, that was all he wanted. That was his priority.

I quickly ran downstairs and bought him the largest sandwich available. When I got back, his whole demeanor changed. He quickly ate the sandwich, and afterward, he became the nicest patient I ever had. He didn't get up again, didn't pull on anything, and we quickly got his blood pressure under control.

To summarize, what I did was not what I was trained to do, but I did what was needed to get the situation under control. I did what was important for my patient. It was his body, his needs, and I did everything to address them. Once his needs were taken care of, we were able to control what was important to us: his blood pressure. As I look back, I am happy with how the situation was resolved. I did what my patient needed, and that is what I was trained for.

Reflection

This is a narrative that highlights the author seeing the patient and using clinical judgment to assess and address their priorities. The patient was agitated because they were hungry, which was contributing to the hypertensive crisis. The author assessed that it was safe for the patient to eat and understood the patient's priorities. Sure enough, once the patient ate, the patient was cooperative because they felt understood, and the author was able to effectively treat the hypertensive crisis. This author truly met the patient "where they are" and used clinical judgment to address a human need and priority.

A potential question related to this narrative may be:

At the beginning of their shift, a nurse receives a report for their daily assignment. Which of the following scenarios should the nurse give first priority:

- **A family member of a post-surgical client with questions.**
- **A client who needs assistance going to the bathroom.**
- **A diabetic client with a blood glucose of 230 mg/dL.**
- **A client with a blood pressure of 270/110 mmHg.**

While all clients are priorities, the nurse must use clinical judgment to prioritize effectively. The last client option is the priority in this case due to the increased blood pressure and potential for increased complications. The diabetic client may be triaged, and another blood glucose level should be taken – which can be delegated to a team member or colleague. The client who needs assistance going to the bathroom is at high risk of falls, but this task can also be delegated. A stable client who has post-surgical questions is not the priority compared to a client who is experiencing a potential hypertensive crisis.

Clinical Judgment: Expert

Narrative by Juliann Altman, MSN, RN, FNP-C, CNOR, RNFA

My nursing career began in 2006 when I became a Licensed Practical Nurse. Since then, I've steadily advanced through the nursing field, earning my RN in 2011, followed by my BSN in 2014, and my MSN in Nursing Executive Leadership in 2021. Along the way, I pursued two post-MSN certificates in Nursing Education and Family Nurse Practitioner. I am also a Certified Nurse Operating Room (CNOR) and a Registered Nurse First Assistant, continually striving to expand my skills and expertise to provide the highest level of care.

I remember a specific time when I was working as an operating room (OR) nurse at a small community hospital. I was seven months pregnant with my son, still pushing through the long hours and unpredictable shifts that came with being on call. That particular night, I had just fallen asleep when I was woken by a phone call from the house supervisor – there was a patient with a bowel obstruction, and I was needed in the OR. It didn't matter that I was pregnant; as an on-call OR nurse, duty came first. Reluctantly, I dragged myself out of bed, dressed in a haze, and made my way to the hospital, not prepared for the emotional toll the night would bring.

When I arrived, I was relieved to see one of my favorite surgical techs. This tech was a seasoned professional who had been working in the OR for decades. She was my constant support during the stressful, chaotic moments of on-call work. I always felt at ease when I was with her – she knew how to handle anything that came our way, whether it was a complex surgery or a hectic night shift. This colleague had been there when I was first learning how to scrub in, always offering guidance and lightheartedness during tough cases.

The hospital at night was quiet. The Ors were essentially a ghost town – dark, isolated, and far from the bustling departments during the day. As on-call staff, we were the only ones in the building, operating in a small world of our own. The team for the night was made up of a circulating nurse (me), a surgical tech, and an anesthesiologist. The patient would be prepped by a post-anesthesia care unit (PACU) nurse before being brought to the OR, but other than that, it was just the three of us until the patient was rolled into the room.

I was informed that the patient had arrived in PACU, so I finished setting up the OR with the tech before heading over to meet him. I called the surgeon to let him know the patient had arrived, but the response was not what I expected. He told me he'd be 20 minutes out. That struck me as odd – he should have already been in the PACU, discussing the case and getting consent. Apparently, one of his partners had relayed information about the patient's CT scan and booked the surgery for him, but now we were stuck waiting.

I went to meet the patient, an 81-year-old veteran, who was in good spirits despite the pain he was experiencing. You would never have guessed he had a bowel obstruction by looking at him – he was cheerful, engaged, and eager to talk. In the brief time I had before the surgeon arrived, we chatted. He told me about his war experiences, his grandchildren, and how excited he was to become a great-grandfather. He even asked about my pregnancy, joking about how life would never be the same once the baby arrived. I felt a deep connection to him. I didn't often get the chance to have these conversations with patients. In the fast-paced world of the operating room, the focus was always on efficiency and precision, and patients usually don't remember us after anesthesia. But with this patient, I found myself deeply moved. He reminded me of my grandfathers, all of whom I had lost by the age of nine.

Talking with him felt like a rare gift, one that I would carry with me through the night.

When the surgeon arrived, we quickly obtained consent, and the patient was wheeled into the OR. The anesthesiologist started prepping, and the tech and the surgeon scrubbed in. I completed the required "timeout" and documented the start time of the surgery. But within minutes, something went terribly wrong. "Hold up," the anesthesiologist called out. "The patient is becoming unstable."

I watched as the anesthesiologist tried to figure out what happened. Suddenly, he shouted, "Someone begin compressions!" The tech, my favorite colleague, ever the pro, immediately broke sterility and began chest compressions. After a few rounds, she gasped for air and asked for relief. I stepped up, took her place, and began compressions over my very pregnant belly. It was exhausting, but I had no choice. The surgical tech was winded, and I couldn't leave her to struggle alone. The anesthesiologist insisted that he could handle it, but I knew we needed more help. I asked the tech to call the PACU nurse for assistance.

When the PACU nurse arrived, we swapped out again for more rounds of compressions. Yet, even with the added help, the patient wasn't stabilizing. I felt a surge of anxiety, but I pushed it aside. The surgeon stood by, watching, offering no help. I asked the PACU nurse if he could stay to help, but he hesitated, saying he shouldn't be there if I hadn't officially called a code. By this point, I was beginning to feel the familiar pangs of abdominal pain from the stress and physical strain. The tech, barely able to catch her breath, was in no better shape. Despite the anesthesiologist's insistence that I hold off, I made the decision and called an overhead code.

Within minutes, the OR was flooded with people – more nurses, more doctors, more help. The patient was stabilized, surgery was postponed, and the surgeon went to speak with the patient's family. The surgical tech and I were left to clean up the room. Exhausted, we finished our duties and headed home at 3 a.m., only to return to the hospital just four hours later to start our day all over again.

As OR nurses, we rarely hear the outcomes of the patients we work on unless we specifically ask. Several hours later, we found out the devastating news – the patient had passed away shortly after being transferred to the ICU. I couldn't shake the connection I had made with him. I had been so wrapped up in our conversation about his grandchildren, his life, and the excitement of impending parenthood that I didn't prepare myself for the inevitable truth that sometimes, despite our best efforts, patients don't make it. I blamed myself for letting myself get attached, for becoming emotionally invested in someone whose life I could not save.

That night, I learned something I hadn't expected – that it's impossible to go through this work without letting some of your heart slip into it. In a job where detachment is often seen as a necessity, I realized that true care isn't something you can easily compartmentalize. No matter how hard we try to keep our distance, sometimes the connections we make are the very things that keep us going. And in the end, even though it was painful, I wouldn't trade those moments of shared humanity for anything.

A few years later, I found myself reflecting on this experience, my perspective shifted as I grew more confident and knowledgeable in my role. For a long time, I carried a sense of resentment toward my job, especially since I felt that nothing came of that night's events. I believed that the patient's death might have been influenced, in part, by the inadequacies of the compressions he was receiving – compressions that I, alongside my colleagues, had been responsible for. But with time and a deeper understanding of my role, I came to realize that I did everything I could physically for that patient. I made the choice to call the code team, despite anesthesia's objections, and that decision, though difficult, was one I stand by. In hindsight, I regret not calling it sooner, when my instincts first told me something was wrong. But as much as I wish I could change that, I know that I can't rewrite the past. What I can do is learn from it – taking that knowledge with me to make better, more confident decisions in the future.

Reflection

Patient safety is the top priority in nursing. Trusting your clinical judgment and instincts is essential – a lesson highlighted in this chapter. We, as nurses, are trained to rely on our assessment skills, and through our careers, they only get better. Use your judgment to ask for help or escalate your concerns or question colleagues' orders. The above scenario regarding the patient coding in the OR is a unique situation. In settings where anesthesia is already present and multiple providers and team members are available, such as intensive care units or peri-operative spaces, codes or rapid responses are not often utilized given the proximity of all team members necessary to stabilize patients. That is potentially why the anesthesiologist in the scenario did not want to call a code. That said, the author relied on their clinical judgment and asked for more help because they didn't feel the situation was improving or as safe as it could have been. The author called a code and did the right thing. We are part of an interprofessional team where not one discipline is the sole decision-maker. Patients and colleagues benefit when there is a conversation about the best course of action. We should always find ourselves working and practicing in a "just culture" where one feels safe and protected to act in patients' best interest and perform within their scope to the best of their ability. The nurse in this narrative was not punished for calling a code in a non-traditional setting where codes don't often occur, but instead, this action potentially prolonged this patient's life and allowed for a more peaceful death for the patient and the family by asking for help to ensure the patient did not expire in the OR while separated from their loved ones.

Although there were no errors made in the narrative above, the authors of this text want to highlight the concept of just culture. The excerpt below highlighting the concept of just culture is taken from an article in the *Gastroenterology Nursing Journal* written by one of this text's editors, Peter Stoffan (2024):

> Albert Wu (2000) is known as the first to document the expression "second victim", meaning the non-patients who are witness to or are involved in an unintentional medical error and feel the anguish, isolation, judgment, shame and possible retributions due to the error. Following the 2000 IOM publication, studies have revealed that punitive and shaming cultures are shown to lead to preventable errors. Because of this, institutions have shifted blaming those who cause unintentional errors to studying the root cause of the error while examining the systems-at-large that led to said error. This mentality and methodology is known as "just culture."
>
> Having a just culture doesn't mean that human errors won't happen. In a just culture, institutions and leaders must consider a few factors when investigating incidents. For example, if we know that someone was impaired on the job or if someone knowingly acted outside of their scope and/or knowingly aimed to cause harm, discipline, or suspension should occur. The National Patient Safety Institute (NPSI) (2023) has created an easy-to-follow diagram including questions to consider when errors are reported:

- Impairment (was the team member impaired?).
- Substitution (would others with the same knowledge have the potential to make the same decisions that led to the error?).
- Intention (was the team member acting with good intention?).

This decision tree, developed by NPSI, is a tool that many institutions have adopted and adapted for their organizational culture. The tool helps leaders determine if team members require coaching, consoling, training, or discipline.

References

National Patient Safety Institute (2023, August 3). *Just culture tool.* https://zdoggmd.com/wp- content/uploads/2018/12/Just-Culture-Tool_NPSF-Version_Adelman_9_22_16.pdf

Stoffan, P. (2024) Intimidation is not the key: Supporting leaders through a just culture framework. *Gastroenterology Nursing*, 47(2): 156–157. https://doi.org/10.1097/SGA.0000000000000080

Wu, A. W. (2000). Medical error: The second victim. The doctor who makes the mistake needs help too. *BMJ*, 320(7237): 726–727. https://doi.org/10.1136/bmj.320.7237.726

Chapter 4

Communication and Documentation: Introduction

Communication is central to who we are as nurses and forms the basis of the nurse-patient relationship, the foundation of all nursing practice. Communication is, of course, both verbal and nonverbal, and both aspects are central to the nursing process. Communication skills are taught in all fundamental nursing courses and enhanced throughout the clinical experiences in basic nursing curricula. As nurses, we learn that there is no such thing as casual conversation in the healthcare environment. Patients will pay close attention to our words and non-verbal communication as their health depends on us as monitors and communicators to the rest of the healthcare team. We are the ones in hospital settings monitoring the patient continuously. Patients trust us and will often share experiences, concerns, fears, thoughts, and even aspects of their personal lives that they have not shared with others.

Documentation is equally important to nurses in carrying out their professional roles and responsibilities. Nurses

DOI: 10.4324/9781003586548-4

are taught that if it is not documented, it did not happen. Documentation is necessary for continuous, coordinated care of patients, providing a means for the nurse to transfer knowledge of the patient's condition and record observations, interventions, and treatments. Nursing documentation, now primarily completed through electronic health records (EHRs), particularly in hospital care, but also in outpatient encounters within healthcare systems, is essential for teamwork among all members of the healthcare team. All formal documentation also serves as a legal record of care provided throughout a patient's hospital stay and/or health system interaction.

The novice nurse recounts her experience with a patient who made a sexual advance and the very positive way in which she handled the communication with the patient by being firm and direct in her verbal and non-verbal communication that his actions were not appropriate. Further, she communicated this interaction to her coworkers and was proactive in subsequently having one other person in the room with her when she provided care to the patient. Yet, the focus of her story is that she did not report the incident to her manager and wonders what would have happened if she had filed a formal complaint. The nurse is well aware of the underreporting of patient abuse due to shame and embarrassment. She recommends that we openly address transgressions in patient behavior, even though she did not do so herself. She learned from this experience, and her reflection was that her communication omission was the major learning for her as a novice nurse.

The beginner professional nurse recounts a story of persistence in her communication with the medical team, at a time in the care system, the night shift, when everyone is stretched and very busy. The nurse notices a significant change in a patient's status and persists in getting the attention of the neurologist and subsequently connects the communication between the radiologist and the neurologist. This story reflects the professional nurse's keen awareness of her responsibility in monitoring the patient's symptoms and, importantly, in persistently communicating these changes to the medical team. An interesting outcome to the story is the former patient approaching the nurse at an outside event and telling her she did not remember the details of what had happened that night on the unit, but she remembered the nurse's voice. And she remembered that the nurse had said to her that she was doing everything that she could to get her home to her family. Words matter!

The intermediate nurse shares a story of a lapse in her documentation that could have led to a negative outcome for the patient. The nurse documented her intervention, a recording that was crucial to the patient's continuous care, but failed to save the documentation. Thus, the documentation did not exist in the record. The positive outcome in this story is the communication between an experienced nurse, who sought out the intermediate nurse even though the nurse was on a lunch break, to clarify the patient's condition and ask whether the documentation was accurate. This astute judgment and nurse-to-nurse communication led to quality patient care through accurate documentation and subsequent intervention.

The proficient nurse was a leader on the patient care unit. She described her intervention in communicating the harmful, abusive behavior of both a patient and the patient's family members. This abusive behavior included negative communication and verbal threats by both the patient and family members. The nurse leader communicated the abusive behavior and threats to the security team at the institution, and it was necessary to restrict visitors to the patient's room. Further, this abusive behavior was documented in the patient's electronic health record so that future care providers would be alerted to the behavior.

The expert nurse recounts a story of inconsistent documentation related to the site of surgery. The nurse noticed the discrepancy in the immediate pre-operative period and was instrumental in getting this corrected immediately before surgery. This story illustrates the attentiveness to details that are extremely important in documentation to avoid medical errors, and the importance of prompt communication within the healthcare team to intervene before the error occurs. The nurse's role as safety officer is recounted through this story.

Communication and Documentation Narrative: Novice

Narrative by Maria Molnar, MSN, RN, FNP-C

Note to the reader – this story reflects on a sexual harassment situation experienced by a nurse from a patient.

I am a nurse practitioner (NP) working in internal medicine in a large hospital system but I worked as a nurse for approximately three years prior to working in the NP role I have now. As I look back on my nursing career, there are innumerable memories that shaped my experience. From spending extra time sitting with patients who didn't have family members visiting them, to cracking jokes with patients to make them laugh, to cheerful times with coworkers, these moments I remember fondly. However, there were also the hard moments, usually being understaffed, caring for more patients than what was considered "safe," doing CPR on a patient that you had fought so hard to keep alive during a shift, and many helpless feelings that come with this profession.

One specific moment that remains with me occurred when I was a new nurse working on a transplant floor. The patients were very high acuity and would be roomed in an intensive care unit (ICU) at any other hospital. Our floor was considered a med-surg floor; thus, our nurse-to-patient ratios were higher than an ICU floor, making the job difficult. This top hospital drew patients in from all over the world to receive world-class service and care. I was caring for a man from a different culture than mine who recently had a large abdominal surgery. His surgery required dressing changes twice per shift during his stay in the hospital. I was entering his room to do his dressing change in the afternoon. His blinds were shut so the room was very dark; he had preferred to keep the lights off and blinds drawn during the day. The sun was still bright through the blinds, so I had enough light to do the dressing change. He spoke limited English, but understood what I was saying to him and could tell me that it was alright that I proceeded with his abdominal dressing change. His wound was massive, vertical from his diaphragm down to his pubic bone, leaking copious amounts of thick white and green fluid. As I was slightly bending over the bed to complete his dressing change, he grabbed my face and tried to kiss me. Thankfully, I was able to turn my head quickly, so his lips landed on my left cheek. I turned, looked at him, mouth agape, cheeks reddened with embarrassment that that event had just happened. His impish grin permeated across his face as he started to laugh. I told him "No!" and that what he did was not ok. I finished the dressing change and left the room.

Having had great relationships with my coworkers, I informed them what had happened. My direct manager had left work that day so there was not a supervisor to immediately report to. At that time, I felt that I handled the situation as best I could; I had told my perpetrator patient "no" and that what he did was not ok. Unfortunately, his reaction was not what I was expecting. He knew what he did was wrong but took pleasure in doing it anyway.

I exited the room and was wracking my brain; could this have been a cultural discrepancy? Was I giving off the impression that I enjoyed this man's company or was I inadvertently flirting? No, none of the above. I was simply doing my job. The thoughts that come to mind after sexual harassment occurs can be hard to describe. Shame is a common emotion victims feel. Embarrassment that such an outlandish act could occur. These emotions make it difficult to bring up to others, especially bosses, managers, or direct supervisors that we report to. Many times, because of these emotions, these acts go unreported, leading to minimal consequences served to perpetrators and thus additional acts by the guilty continuing to take place. Sadly, then, sexual harassment can easily become part of the "norm" of what nurses can experience doing the one job they worked so hard for.

The additional times I had to enter his room that day to give him medications or to answer his call light, I had another colleague willingly go in the room with me. Looking back, I am glad to have had such great coworkers; we really functioned as a team unit and stood with each other in turbulent times.

By the time my next shift rolled around, the patient had been discharged. I never specifically told my manager what had happened, as I believed there would likely be no repercussions for the patient, as he had left the hospital. Maybe one of my colleagues had spoken to my boss. Regardless, the situation was not discussed again. I view this as a failure, and I should have informed my boss as to what had happened. Maybe nothing would have come from it, but by stepping up, being brave, and voicing the truth, change can occur.

I write about this experience not because I am proud of it, but because I feel that it needs to be discussed more in nursing. Nursing, a heavily female-populated profession, is established on the principles of caring for patients. This compassionate career sometimes forces nurses to put others' needs before their own. In this context, the ideal "patient's first," drastically fails nurses. We expect our job to be safe and we should be treated as professionals, not as objects to be taken advantage of. Sadly, even if a nurse is to experience such aggression, she can respond appropriately by telling the patient that his actions are not appropriate, but what are the repercussions for the patient? The hospital system will not discharge him or her without proper medical care. It may be a stern warning or a slap on the wrist, but will that keep the perpetrator from doing it again? In contrast, sexual harassment in a typical workplace environment can result in termination of the perpetrator. The perceived power dynamics between the nurse and the patient are vastly different. Nurses are often perceived to service the patient and give the patient what he or she wants or needs. What is even more disheartening is how common sexual harassment is in nursing.

In retrospect, I wish I would have reported the incident to my manager. As nurses, we must stand up and report the abuses when they occur. As nursing leaders, we need to create a safe, transparent, and open environment, listen to what our fellow colleagues are experiencing and be willing to enact changes to keep the workplace environment safe. This will hopefully assist in preserving the longevity of the profession.

Reflection

This author is brave for sharing a story that is unfortunately more common than one may think. It is true that there is a power dynamic and energy transference between our patients and us nurses. This predatory behavior by the patient (blinds down, lights off, waiting until the nurse was defenseless while performing a clinical dressing change procedure to take advantage of the nurse) is unacceptable. The nurse took swift action to say "no" and admonish the behavior but, of course, relied on her nursing instinct to finish the dressing change before leaving the room. While the nurse may have wanted to forfeit her duties in taking care of this patient, she showed her bravery and professionalism once again and carried through with providing care for this patient. The nurse acted appropriately by ensuring a nurse colleague would enter the patient's room with her for the rest of the shift to ensure her physical and psychological safety.

What else could have been done by this nurse? *We pose this question not to suggest this author was wrong in any way, but as a reflective/simulative exercise in preparing you, the reader, for how to act should an event like this ever occur in your practice.*

The nurse may have called Security and Patient Services immediately and asked for a Security officer and a Patient Services Representative to speak with the patient and relay that the behavior was unacceptable and not permissible. While patients are protected, as the author states, this does not give anyone the right to disrespect or harass the clinical team members who are there to provide care. Having non-clinical team members communicate this with patients is a tactic that can help set boundaries and standards of respect.

Reporting such behavior is imperative. Whether or not you feel comfortable speaking to a supervisor or colleague, many healthcare systems/facilities have reporting mechanisms that allow team members to report activities of assault (inclusive of physical, verbal, emotional assaults) anonymously. This helps the human resources, security, and leadership teams examine systems that can be created and/or deployed to appropriately support the vulnerable population that is healthcare workers. Many systems/facilities also have counseling resources available to healthcare workers that provide free and anonymous psychological support. Make sure you take time to know what resources are available to you at your place of work.

Communication and Documentation Narrative: Beginner

Narrative by Kelly Varga, BSN, RN, CEN

As a newer nurse you never know how much of an impact you will have on someone's life. I had just started on a telemetry unit that specialized in strokes. I had a few years of experience in long-term care and a brain injury rehab, but my patient's illnesses were chronic in nature. This was my first true acute care experience. I was fresh off orientation and eager to be the best I could be. I worked the night shift which left us with limited resources at times. On this particular night, all the resources lined up perfectly for me and my patient.

I received a report from the emergency department that I was getting a 43-year-old woman that suffered a stroke earlier in the day. The patient had stepped out of her car and fell on her face, causing a large hematoma on her forehead and scalp. Due to the large hematoma she was not a candidate for any type of intervention involving thrombolytics. I met the patient in the room and did my initial assessment. I proceeded to carry on with what I was doing with other patients but was drawn back into her room. I completed another stroke scale on her and now my number was different. I understand that the number can be different from time to time but it seemed as if the patient's symptoms were completely different and the stroke was evolving. I proceeded to exit the room and the neurologist was walking down the hall. She immediately put her hand up saying "Kelly I'm really busy tonight, I don't think I can take on another case." I pleaded with her that this is urgent and I really needed her to see this patient. Reluctantly she accepted the case and thanked me later for being persistent.

I went to the nurses' station for a phone call from the reading radiologist. He was adding an addendum onto the CT scan that the patient had a large vessel occlusion and that it was possibly retrievable through intervention. I proceeded to go back to the patient's room where the neurologist was completing her assessment and I asked the neurologist to speak with the radiologist who was on the phone. Within a quick thirteen minutes, the transfer of this patient from our hospital to a trauma and stroke hospital that had the resources to treat this patient had been arranged and the critical care transport nurse was standing in front of me for report. I completed the transfer and my stroke coordinator followed up with the case beyond our hospital. I visited the patient when she came back to the rehabilitation unit within our facility; however, she did not remember me. I didn't take offense to this as with any traumatic brain injury there can be memory lapses around the traumatic event.

Fast forward five months and I am sitting at my daughter's swim meet, cheering on her and her teammates. I received a tap on my shoulder and the woman standing next to me using a cane asked, "Are you a nurse?" My heart sank. This was the same woman that sat in front of me months ago with an evolving stroke. She continued to tell me that she doesn't remember much of what happened that night or the weeks following; however, she remembered my voice. She remembered me telling her "I am doing everything I can do to get you home to your family." Those words stuck with her as well as my voice. Our daughters competed together that summer and I am very happy to say that I was part of the reason why she is able to have the quality of life that she has to share with her family.

Reflection

This narrative perfectly exemplifies the nurses' voice and impact on patient outcomes when we raise our voices and speak up. What would have happened if this author had not performed a second neuro assessment? Without this clinical intervention, the patient may not have made it to her daughter's swim meet that same year. Respectful and assertive communication in clinical settings is necessary in order to speak up and advocate on behalf of our patients. There is a program offered through the Agency for Healthcare Research and Quality (AHRQ) called TeamSTEPPS that stands for Team Strategies & Tools to Enhance Performance and Patient Safety (AHRQ, 2025). This training centers around assertive communication strategies in order to drive crucial conversations to advocate for patient safety. As nurses, we are leaders on the interprofessional team, and oftentimes are better informed regarding patient conditions due to the privilege of spending more time with the patient at the bedside. We use our clinical judgment to assess and constantly re-assess our patients; therefore, we frequently have the most up-to-date picture of how our patients are actually doing. TeamSTEPPS recommends that nurses adopt this way of thinking: "CUS" or "I am Concerned, I am Uncomfortable, this is a Safety issue"(AHRQ, 2023).

This author spoke up. This author did not take "no" for an answer when they knew something was happening and something was different from what it was in a prior assessment. As nurses, our clinical judgment guides our actions. A question related to this narrative may be:

A patient was recently admitted after an unwitnessed fall at home to the medical-surgical unit on a previous shift, less than an hour ago. The previous nurse reported that all vital signs were within normal limits and the patient was alert and oriented x 4 (person,

place, time, and event). You enter the patient's room and assess that the patient is disoriented and is presenting with unilateral facial drooping. Your best next action is:

- **Perform a mini-mental exam.**
- **Call the neurologist to provide updates.**
- **Call the Stroke Team.**
- **Call the patient's family to ask if they would like to come for a visit.**

The patient in the above scenario may be experiencing a stroke. Unilateral weakness, as displayed by facial drooping, may be a clinical indicator of an active stroke occurring. As nurses, we must escalate concerns immediately, and if there is a suspected stroke, the best course of action is to alert the stroke team. Treatment for a stroke is most effective when activated as soon as possible. Performing a mini-mental exam may be more appropriate in post-stroke patients to assess post-stroke cognition. Calling a primary team to provide an update can be done, but only after activating a rapid response stroke team first. Activating the stroke team first will activate any facility-based algorithms and can expedite treating the patient and potentially improve the patient's outcome. Lastly, communicating with the family during a time of emergency is important, but advocating for emergency clinical treatment takes precedence in this scenario in order to potentially save a patient's life.

References

Agency for Healthcare Research and Quality. (2020, January). Pocket guide: TeamSTEPPS. Agency for Healthcare Research and Quality. Retrieved May 15, 2025, from https://www.ahrq.gov/teamstepps/instructor/essentials/pocketguide.html

Communication and Documentation Narrative: Competent

Narrative by Anonymous

I was a few years into my nursing career when I transferred to the Post-Anesthesia Care Unit (PACU) or Recovery Room. I had a few friends who worked there and thought the idea of working in the unit that gets to take care of patients immediately after surgery and anesthesia sounded fun and like a great learning experience. It was on the unit tour during my interview that I learned the phrase "controlled chaos" because that is exactly what the PACU can be. So many people coming in and out of a big open room with no doors, just curtains. Barely arousable patients entering the recovery room on stretchers with a team surrounding them (usually physicians, anesthesia providers – CRNAs or MDs, and others) and a few hours later, the same patient would be alert and oriented and being wheeled off to another unit once recovered from anesthesia, and sometimes, the patients may be walking out of the room to go home just hours after arriving.

I knew I had a lot to learn about the anesthetic agents and how it affects the body at different ages in addition to a myriad of new surgeries I hadn't encountered or learned about in nursing school or in my previous unit experience. The acuity level was higher than I was used to as well as the PACU can sometimes be an intensive care unit (ICU) holding area if there weren't any ICU beds available. This meant that I needed to learn about ventilators, high-flow oxygen, medication drips, and different tests that these patients would require to effectively and safely manage their care.

One type of surgery that was new to me as a clinician was kidney transplant surgeries. I would recover both cadaver transplants and living transplants. Both types of surgery were exciting and unique in the post-surgical care implications.

Both required strict ins and outs documentation to ensure the kidney was being flushed and perfused appropriately. The living transplants required much more fluid replacement than the cadaver transplants due to the "freshness" of the organ. Providers would order 1:1 fluid replacement…meaning that if the urine output was 500mL for one hour, the next hour the patient would need to receive 500mL of IV fluids. So, if you were the nurse for these patients, you were constantly assessing and documenting the urine output and ensuring the IV fluid replacement was appropriately given and documented.

One shift, I went on break while caring for a living transplant patient and I gave a report to a seasoned nurse colleague. I had thought that I had documented the previous hour's urine output and appropriately documented that the next hour of fluid input would be the 1:1 replacement as ordered by the providers. About ten minutes into my break, the nurse found me in the break room eating my lunch and apologized for interrupting my break but asked me to join her at the bedside for a moment to clarify something. I joined my colleague at the bedside and she asked me clarify the patient's input and output. I realized that my charting had never saved and did not capture the previous hour's urine output. Therefore, this nurse saw a large fluid bolus programmed in the IV pump without understanding the previous hour's urine output. This more experienced nurse had a decision to make:

- Stop the bolus and wait an hour since no urine output was documented the previous hour (*which can happen with kidney transplants, but more likely with cadaver transplants as they take more time to produce urine…).*

or

- Come find me to clarify and avoid limiting the patient's fluid unnecessarily.

This experienced nurse knew that fluid replacement is crucial for kidney transplant patients and opted to find me and clarify my documentation.

I learned a valuable lesson that day. Save save save your work. There is a phrase I hear a lot in nursing – "if it isn't documented, it didn't happen." But more than that, I learned to ensure documentation is airtight and clear for anyone who is caring for the patient after me. This lack of documentation could have jeopardized the patient's new kidney and caused a never event. I am thankful for this nurse colleague of mine who, rather than making an assumption based on the lack of documentation, chose to use her nursing judgment to ensure the patient had a safe and optimal outcome.

Reflection

This narrative highlights how effective communication and documentation are paramount in the care of our patients. It also highlights how communication and documentation are different. The author gave a handoff to the colleague and potentially mentioned the previous hour's output and why the IV pump was programmed the way it was, but because the documentation was not reflective of the patient's condition, there was a gap. This nurse author learned a valuable lesson to ensure documentation is airtight. This could have resulted in a terrible outcome for the patient, but thanks to the more experienced nurse who clarified the gap in documentation, the patient had a positive outcome.

A potential question related to this scenario is:

The post-operative nurse understands that all of the following are priorities for the post-operative renal transplant recipient patient except:

- **Adequate intravenous fluids as ordered by the provider.**
- **NPO status for the first 24 hours postoperatively.**
- **Preparing the patient for a renal echo test.**
- **Ensuring family communication occurs.**

The nurse should prioritize appropriate intravenous fluids to ensure renal perfusion is occurring. Similarly, a renal echo or renal ultrasound should be ordered in the immediate post-operative setting to ensure there are no obstructions or damage to the new kidney. Appropriate family communication is another priority, as families and loved ones will be anxious about the status of their loved one. Patients also have the right and need for contact with their loved ones. NPO status is not a mandate for post-operative patients. Patients should be advanced to clear liquids postoperatively as tolerated and as ordered by providers once patients have recovered from anesthesia and have no risk for aspiration.

Communication and Documentation Narrative: Proficient

Narrative by Katherine Babcock, MPA, BSN, RN, CPAN

As a nurse leader, I am responsible not only for the safe and quality care of the patients in the unit where I lead, but also for the safe and quality environment of care for the team members for which I have the privilege to lead. The healthcare environment has changed over the years…a time not too long ago, we used to (wrongfully) limit visitation from families and loved ones in acute settings thinking we were protecting our patients from distractions and shielding visitors from a chaotic hospital environment. How wrong we were. Having families, loved ones, and visitors for patients has been proven to improve patient outcomes. There are times, however, when visitation rights must be revisited or at dire times be revoked.

There was a patient recently in the unit who was extremely abusive to the nursing team members. The patient would make threats, physically assault the nurses by hitting or grabbing the nurses' arms when providing care and use profanities toward any providing care for this patient. We enlisted the help of the family members of this patient to assist with de-escalating the poor behavior. Within the first hour of the family being at the bedside, it became clear that the family was empowering the patient to behave in this manner. They too were angry about the patient's condition and would take it out on the care team. The family would also make verbal threats and assaults toward the interprofessional team members. As the leader of the unit, I knew something immediate would have to occur.

We enlisted the help from our patient services and security partners to stress to the patient and visitors that such behavior would not be tolerated. Hospitals are a place for healing and any negative or threatening behavior interrupts the care and healing environment we work hard to create and protect. After continued threats from the family toward the nurses, we unfortunately had to refuse visitation from the family to protect the physical and emotional safety of the care team. After the patient continued to attempt to physically assault the nurses, we communicated with our security and leadership team members that constant observation would need to occur.

Additionally, we determined that we needed to somehow flag this patient's electronic medical record for the future to protect any other care team members of this inappropriate and unsafe behavior. Upon handoff to the next unit, we ensured that the receiving care team understood the risk in taking care of this patient and the importance of the constant observation by Security. We, at all times, must protect the safety of our colleagues. We were successful in flagging the patient's chart stating the patient caused employee harm so the next time the patient was admitted, the team would be aware and would be able to implement safety precautions for themselves to prevent it from happening again.

It was a tough situation but we worked together to ensure our communication with the family and patient was appropriate and safety-oriented. We also worked together to ensure our documentation reflected this unfortunate behavior and could help prevent others from receiving such negative and unsafe interruptions in the way they provide care.

Reflection

Earlier in this chapter, we have a narrative that discusses inappropriate sexual behavior from patients toward the nursing team. In this narrative, we have another example of inappropriate verbal and physical behavior, but this time, seemingly rooted in anger. Both examples are unacceptable, and as the nurse author says, they interrupt the way we provide care to our patients. In this example, the nurse leader recognized that an escalation of communication was needed and enlisted the partnership of Security and Patient Services. After the family also presented signs of abuse toward the care team, the leader in this narrative recognized that creative documentation was needed. What would stop this behavior from happening again in future circumstances? They worked with the informatics team to ensure the patient's chart was flagged to protect the safety of any future care teams. This was an innovative thought by the nurse leader and care team. We may only think of the current state of our patients when we think about communication and documentation, but this team was thinking ahead for the betterment of all.

A sample question related to this scenario may be:

The nurse understands that the following statements communicated by the patient trigger an immediate interprofessional meeting with the patient including patient services:

- **"I'm so angry and I don't want to be here. I hate hospitals."**
- **"If you give me that medicine, I'll spit it out."**
- **"The other nurse better not come in this room or else."**
- **"If you don't do what I ask, I'll call my lawyer."**

The first phrase reflects a patient who may be scared and frustrated by their current prognosis. This may trigger the nurse to begin a therapeutic listening moment for the patient to communicate what is on the patient's mind and how the primary nurse may assist in relieving any fears or frustrations. The second phrase related to medications should also trigger the nurse to adequately communicate what the patient's medications are for. If at that time, perhaps a conversation with the providers regarding medication refusal should occur so the care team can pivot accordingly. The last phrase reflects a patient who may be frustrated and not understand what the nurse's role is. Although the patient is threatening to call their lawyer, they may do so, and it is within their rights to communicate with their advisers. This threat is not a threat *toward* the nurse. The nurse may want to communicate this conversation with the care team to provide an update that the patient is frustrated. This may also trigger the nurse to sit with the patient to fully understand what their goals and understanding are of their prognosis. The third statement, when the patient makes a vague threat about another nurse, is threatening and could potentially escalate quickly; therefore, the nurse should involve the nursing leadership and patient services team to identify if this patient could become violent and unsafe toward the care team.

Communication and Documentation Narrative: Expert

Narrative by Anonymous

Working as a pre-operative nurse is a major responsibility. Some may think it is "just getting a patient ready for surgery" but the role is so much bigger than that. Yes, the pre-operative nurse is the sometimes the first face patient sees in their hospital stay and of course that means setting a tone for the entire hospital course. Being a friendly face, answering questions, providing post-operative education pre-operatively, reassuring families and loved ones, and being the logistical source of truth for all things surgery-related comes with the territory... but SAFETY is the biggest piece of the role.

I remember a recent case that had I not been there reviewing the pre-operative clinic-based documentation, a patient's surgery could have gone terribly wrong. When a patient comes to the ambulatory surgery unit, it is the pre-operative nurses' role to ensure all documentation from the clinic matches the surgery that is scheduled. Their history and physical, pre-operative anesthesia clearance notes, *consent forms, etc...all must be appropriate and match exactly the patients' surgical booking.

**To note – often times consents are done day of surgery but ideally they are done before the day of surgery. At the very least, unless it is an emergency surgery, the procedure must be discussed with the patient prior to day of surgery to ensure the patient has enough time to consider the benefits and risks and is appropriately informed.*

Back to pre-operative documentation matching day-of surgery documentation – if a patient is admitted for a left-leg surgery, the pre-operative history and physical must indicate a left-leg surgery. The consent must say left leg. The pre-anesthesia evaluation must be present. The surgical booking in the Operating Room (OR) Manager tool in the electronic medical record must be for the left leg. The surgeon must come to the patient's bedside and mark the patient's left leg with a surgical marking pen day of surgery and review the patient's consent form to ensure all is correct and the surgery may proceed. (Then of course, in the OR, there is a whole other set of safety checks known as Universal Protocol including the Time-Out procedure when all team members stop what they are doing to verify it is the correct patient, correct procedure, correct indication, correct side, and any allergies or other medical information.)

One patient sticks out to me recently and it was a patient who was admitted for a cataract extraction or removal from their left eye. All pre-operative documents were in place so after welcoming the patient and admitting them to their pre-operative space in the unit, I started my document review. The pre-operative history and physical indicated a cataract in the left eye but the surgical ophthalmologist's consent form was for the right eye. I immediately stopped everything I was doing and called the surgeon. The surgeon came directly to the bedside and reviewed the pre-operative consent and recognized the error. We immediately initiated a new consent form for the correct (left) eye and the patient and witness filled out their section. This said, an informed consent should not be done on day of surgery because informed consents should not be performed when a patient may be worried or distracted. Because the original wrong consent was a typo error, the patient understood and was thankful of our safety protocols that kept this from occurring. The surgeon then surgically marked the left side of the patient's face and we continued prepping the patient for surgery.

Had I not stopped during my pre-operative checks, this would have been remedied and reviewed intra-operatively...but what would have happened if I didn't check the pre-operative documentation thoroughly and it WASN'T checked intra-operatively. I felt very confident and proud of myself as the patient's advocate. As nurses, it is our responsibility to be each of our patients' safety officers and we do this through our communication and documentation.

Reflection

This narrative highlights the importance of our communication and documentation. We must remain diligent because our patients' lives are our responsibilities...not just in the perioperative spaces, but in all areas where we provide care. The way we document and communicate our patients' statuses could change a person's life forever. There is a reason this nurse relied on reviewing the patient's pre-operative documentation in the history and physical rather than just asking the patient, "what side is your cataract surgery today?" Sometimes patients are nervous and would just say yes to a question or be distracted and say right eye rather than the correct left eye. Maybe this patient ultimately would need both eyes operated on for cataract removal, but on this specific day, the patient was prepped for left-eye surgery. If the nurse in this narrative had asked the patient, the patient could have given the wrong information, which highlights the importance of checking the documentation and communicating effectively. We, as nurses, must be critical thinkers at all times to protect and advocate for our patients through our communication and documentation.

A potential question related to this narrative could be:

Which of the below is not a mandatory pre-operative safety check that must occur prior to the patient entering the operating room?

- **Updated history and physical within the previous 30 days.**
- **Completed surgical informed consent.**
- **Patient address updated appropriately in the electronic medical record.**
- **Surgical marking performed by the Surgeon.**

While the patient's address should be updated in the electronic medical record upon each admission, this is not a safety check related to perioperative surgery. The history and physical, consent, and surgical marking are mandatory to occur pre-operatively prior to the patient entering the operating room.

Chapter 5

Culture and Spirituality: Introduction

Holism is foundational to the nursing discipline and thus, professional nursing practice. Within this holistic perspective, nurses integrate an understanding of all dimensions of persons and their environments. This holistic perspective includes the cultural and spiritual aspects of care and the understandings of individuals as influenced by their culture and their spiritual dimensions. It is important to note that this aspect of spirituality does not denote religion but is a broader concept reflective of an understanding of the totality of the universe and humanity. As reflected in these nurses' stories, the spiritual aspects of care are often most evident at the end of life, a time of reflection when a person tries to understand the meaningfulness of the human experience. Often, this is also a time to reflect on family and cultural experiences, as preparations for dying and death are difficult for all involved. Even though care is centered on the patient, the nurse also must be cognizant of the family's wishes, as family members are an important cultural component of the patient's experience of life.

DOI: 10.4324/9781003586548-5

The novice nurse describes her experience as a new graduate nurse who was assigned to care for an individual who had chosen comfort care after months of extensive medical interventions that were not entirely successful. He acknowledged that he was in the final stages of life. The story reflects the holistic care that the nurse provided to the patient during his final minutes, acknowledging his wishes and understanding the loss of life for this individual. The relationship that this nurse had with the patient is artfully described, including the music that accompanied the care and the continued communication with the patient even after he had been pronounced dead. In this reflection, the nurse also acknowledges that she had to accept the family members and their reaction to the patient's decision for comfort care. Our families are part of our cultural context, and while family dynamics must be understood, in this situation, the care of the patient was most important and thus the center of the nurse's intervention.

The story of the beginner nurse also centers on the nurse-patient relationship at the end of life. This patient was also aware that she was at the end of life and acknowledged this to the nurse. In this scenario, the nurse was less ready than the patient but was open to learning from the patient's experience and the patient's spirituality (and religious expressions). As this author describes, engaging in spiritual conversation with patients is deeply meaningful and reflects the bond of humanity that is so important in professional nursing practice.

The story of the proficient nurse is told from the perspective of a palliative care advanced practice nurse. By nature of the practice, the nurse and the patients are addressing the patient's reality that life is coming to an end. This awareness serves as a foundation for the nurse-patient relationship and makes it possible for the nurse and patient to directly address end-of-life wishes and concerns. This proficient nurse was astute in leading care at the patient's pace, asking open-ended questions that allowed the patient to express concerns about the recent absence of religion in his life. He was able to share his spiritual distress, and the nurse prayed with him, with his permission. By listening to the patient's story, the nurse was able to assist him in resolving his spiritual distress.

The competent nurse intervenes in a holistic manner to address not only the patient's needs at the end of life but also the needs of the patient. The nurse builds trust by tuning into the family's cultural values for classical music, introducing the playing of music while providing care for the patient. Throughout this long period of care of the patient, this tie to the patient/family experience was comforting and therapeutic, and assisted all involved in understanding the complexity and meaningfulness of the human experience.

The expert nurse has, over decades, developed a deep understanding of the cultural and thus the holistic nature of nursing. Her experiences among those from other cultures, both in the United States and in other countries, provide a rich understanding of the cultural and spiritual aspects of professional nursing practice. This story is directly centered on the cultural aspects of public health nursing and the learning that occurred for the nurse as much as for those who were the recipients of care, the community.

Culture and spirituality are intertwined in the care we provide as nurses. Knowledge of these dimensions is as important as knowledge of the mind and body, the physiology and the psychology of the health and illness experience. As professional nurses, we build our holistic care in ways that are meaningful to patients, families, and communities, and in the process, we become better humans...better at understanding and valuing the humanity of all.

Culture and Spirituality Narrative: Novice

Narrative by Cait Hogan, BSN, RN

Note: this narrative may be triggering for some, as it mentions death and memories of caring for those during the Covid-19 pandemic

I have been specializing in critical care nursing for over five years. I am a resource and leader at the bedside within my unit. I am also a trained Skin Care Resource Nurse, Geriatrics Resource Nurse, Oncology Resource Nurse, and Chemotherapy Nurse. I have several certifications specific to ICU nursing. Throughout my career, I've had the privilege of working with a variety of patients, from high acuity, unstable, intensive care patients to outpatient procedural patients. This has provided me with a wide-ranging perspective on patient care and the critical role that leadership and professionalism play in our daily work. Over the years, I have worked with interprofessional teams, collaborated on patient-centered initiatives, and learned the importance of fostering both individual and collective growth in nursing practice.

In 2020, I began my career as a new graduate nurse in the Medical ICU (MICU) during the height of the COVID-19 pandemic. I immediately found myself caring for the sickest patients, witnessing many deaths, and participating in new and innovative – often frightening – research, interventions, and therapies. It was isolating and overwhelming. During the second wave of COVID, hospitals began allowing one visitor per patient and students to return to the bedside. Prior to that, the units were staffed by a rotating team of travel nurses, new grad nurses, and even the National Guard, all attempting to support overburdened community hospital systems. We have lost many nurses to COVID, mental illness, and burnout.

On a typical night shift, I changed into my scrubs, swapped my shoes, tied my hair back with a scrub cap, and put on my prescription safety glasses. The N95 mask left an indentation on my nose that has never fully faded, so I also grabbed a foam pad to ease the pressure. I left my personal stethoscope—given to me as a gift for being accepted into nursing school—in my locker. We only used disposable ones. As I received handoff report, regardless of if I was coming or going, I would see multiple morgue carts pass by, a grim reminder of the toll the pandemic was taking on all of us.

One particular night shift, I had a student with me. She was in her early twenties, eager and positive, hoping to pursue pediatrics. I hadn't even been a nurse a year before students and new orientees were given to me due to the volume of experienced nurses leaving the bedside. This was her critical care rotation. She once confided that she had told her mom she didn't think I ever took a bathroom break. We had spent several weeks together, and she was beginning to see the emotional weight of the job.

We received a report on two patients: one was waiting for transport to the morgue, and the other, after months in the hospital and weeks in the MICU, was ready to transition to Comfort Care after his children had decided to visit him one last time. His condition was dire—his lung tumor had grown large enough to be visible on the side of his chest. Despite months of life-saving interventions, the prognosis was poor, even with extraordinary interventions such as intubation. He had been battling COVID-19 since October 2020 and, with the support of the healthcare team, had made the decision to shift his care focus to comfort.

This patient had several children, who had all declined to visit him or have any involvement in his care. Until two made the decision to come tonight, but they did not want to be present during the transition to Comfort Care. The children gowned and masked, then sat in silence with only the sound of folk country music filling the room. Our plan was to notify the resident once they left so we could begin the transition orders for his Comfort Care.

Around 10 p.m., they left without speaking to us. I entered the room with my student, asked the patient if he was in any pain, he declined, and then asked if he was ready for the transition, and he nodded. I paged the resident, who released the Comfort Care orders. We prepared the Hydromorphone drip, gathered the necessary supplies, and had the respiratory therapist join us. I made sure my student was emotionally prepared for the situation and reassured her that she could step out at any time if needed. I again went over the plan before we donned our PPE and double-gloved.

Once we started the Hydromorphone drip, the respiratory therapist removed the patient's BiPAP mask. I performed oral care with mouth swabs, turned on the music, and we held his hand as his breathing slowed. Soon, his chest stopped rising altogether, and I could no longer feel a pulse. I instructed my student to place her yellow disposable stethoscope next to mine on his chest. As I held the patient's hand with my right and my stethoscope with my left, we listened to his last heartbeat. We never knew this man, yet we shared in his final moments. I silenced the alarms and checked his pulse and pupils before paging the resident to pronounce him dead. His time of death was 11:36 p.m. Death, during this time, was often a swift process.

In a brief moment of calm, I asked my student if she felt ready to perform morgue care on our previous patient. As swift a process death was, there seemed to be even less time for grieving. The scent of body bags is something I'll never forget—the same scent as pool floaties. By this time in the pandemic, we only had bariatric-sized bags left. When we opened one, the familiar smell of summer and childhood swirled around the room. I have not been able to visit a pool since without being transported back to those isolation rooms.

I took a moment to explain to my student that everyone finds their own ritual for loss, and this act of caring for a patient after their death could be a part of that. I shared with her that I find value in performing morgue care because it allows me to offer one last act of kindness and care to my patient, even if we hadn't known them long. We gathered our supplies, donned our PPE, and closed the isolation door behind us. As we prepared the patient, a country folk cover of "You've Got a Friend in Me" played softly. I referred to the patient by name and explained to him that we were about to clean him up. I thanked him for allowing us to care for him.

While removing his gown, I found an unlit cigarette between his fingers. I carefully removed it and placed it on the counter. I told my student that we'd return it once we finished. I also joked, I wouldn't risk a curse on my 5/5 night shifts by taking a cigarette from a dead man's hand, especially one given as a last act of kindness from his estranged children when he was most vulnerable. Once we finished cleaning him, I thanked him one more time and verbalized as I returned the cigarette to his fingers. I then tied his toe tag and zipped the body bag up. It's a small but meaningful gesture, something the news never mentions; generally, nursing staff are the ones who tie the toe tags and zip the body bags of those who die in hospitals and/or care facilities. It's our final act of care. We carefully doffed our PPE, performed hand hygiene, and placed our N95s in brown bags for reuse. I texted management that the body was ready for transport and checked in with my student one last time before answering the phone for the report on the already pended patient from the ED, ready to take this bed once emptied.

This experience reinforced the need to hold space for empathy, not only for our patients but for ourselves and colleagues. As an ICU nurse, much of our focus is on saving lives and preventing death. I learned that nursing care and high-stress situations are not just about making clinical decisions; it's about balancing the needs of the patients with the well-being of the team. I also learned that professionalism includes maintaining composure and providing moral support to others, especially when the pressure is at its peak. When someone is admitted to the hospital, then to the ICU, they lose a lot of autonomy. As nurses, we are not only advocates but champions for our patients' autonomy when they cannot exert their own.

Furthermore, I gained a deeper understanding of the importance of self-awareness in nursing. Families are messy and complicated. Part of my nursing care does not include judging a critically ill man or his family. Recognizing my own limitations, seeking support when needed, and empowering my team with the resources and encouragement they required were crucial in making this experience a success. I do not need to have all the answers. Nursing is not always about providing education. Many times, nursing is just existing with a person, supporting, and caring for them at their most vulnerable.

Reflection

This narrative is a stark reminder of the ebb and flow of life and the privilege we have as nurses to see both the beginning and end of patients' lives. This author, though reflecting on a time as a novice nurse, writes with compassion and showcases the professionalism demanded of the discipline of nursing during a most difficult time. This narrative highlights the amazing culture of the nursing disciplines and the many demands and rewards nurses receive, but also the aspect of considering a patient's culture as they transition from life to death.

There are some key components of this narrative that touch upon the aspect of culture and spirituality as it relates to emergency mandates and protocols, end-of-life, and post-mortem care. As nurses, it is our duty to give back to the discipline of nursing through a culture of learning. This novice nurse at the time of this experience may not have felt ready to precept a student nurse, but because of the emergency mandate and protocol in place during the COVID-19 (SARS-CoV-2) pandemic, many nurses and professionals were required to improvise and respond to an unprecedented trigger. This narrative also discusses end-of-life care and how difficult a process that can be…to begin a medication on a patient that will intentionally decrease the respiratory drive for a patient to allow a peaceful transition from life to death is difficult. The fact that the author was focused on checking in on the student nurse is admirable, but one must ask, who was checking in on this nurse, as she was new to practice herself. Lastly, the narrative mentions post-mortem care, which is indeed an aspect of nursing care that is often left out of textbooks. The author never judges the family or patient for not visiting prior to this last day of the patient's life. The author also doesn't judge the patient or family for placing a cigarette in the patient's hand, but instead recognizes that this is part of that family's specific culture. Though we know smoking is bad for one's health, perhaps for this family, the nurse understands that smoking was a habit that this family participated in together. As an aside, nurses should always provide smoking cessation materials, resources, and support for all patients and understand that this particular incident is unique and special. The nurse understood that this patient may have missed smoking while in the hospital, and the family was able to make a small gesture of love during the final hours in a moment of connection. Culture is different for all, and it is the responsibility and privilege of the nurse to seek to understand that culture, assess, and support. This nurse did not, nor should not, support smoking for anyone; however, she understood that at the end of life, an unlit cigarette provided a potential moment of levity, comfort, and connection unique to this family unit's culture.

A potential question related to this narrative may be:

A nurse understands a terminally ill patient has orders for a Hydromorphone IV drip and other medications that will make communication with the patient and family members difficult once initiated. The patient's family members have not wanted to visit the patient during the hospital stay until today. After introducing themselves to the family upon arrival, what question is the most appropriate?

- **"Did you know how sick the patient is?"**
- **"Is there anything I can do to make you comfortable while I start this medication?"**
- **"Has the primary team communicated with you about how the patient is doing and do you have any questions about the patient?"**
- **"What can I do for you during this very difficult time?"**

The first question may be blaming and is, therefore, inappropriate. The second question assumes the patient's family understands what medication you are starting and is, therefore, not the most successful. The last question is a good question to consider; however, the nurse does not know that the family members understand this is a difficult time. The third question is the most appropriate first question to ask to appropriately assess what has been communicated to the family members and allows an open dialogue to begin so the nurse can assess the cultural needs of the patient's family members during this transitional time.

Culture and Spirituality Narrative: Beginner

Narrative by Melanie Walter, RN

In school, I had been introduced to so many options in nursing, it felt overwhelming. After commencement, I began working on a medical/surgical floor for two years. Unbeknownst to me, an inpatient nursing foundation would later fuel my desire to reduce preventable emergency room visits and hospitalizations. After two years of bedside nursing, I found myself in family medicine, a significant culture shift, but ultimately the correct choice.

I have continued my professional calling in ambulatory nursing for the past decade. I am team lead at an ambulatory clinic in Ohio, providing care in family medicine, express care, and multiple specialties. I find fulfillment in getting to know the person behind the patient, guiding people to achieve goals they may not have thought possible, breaking barriers, teaching necessary skills to manage and cope with disease, and having many laughs and tears along the way. Gaining wisdom through my years, I have found that nursing is a challenging journey, the full embrace of which is not comprehended upon commencement. The footprint that remains after a nurse treads upon their path will remain for generations. I certainly did not expect the degree to which that realization has happened for me.

Over the years, I often think back fondly to the first gift I ever accepted from a patient. I was working as a new nurse on the medical/surgical floor, and I was caring for a person named Lola. Lola had terminal cancer, had lost all her hair, was in pain, and was emaciated. Once, on night shift rounding, I found Lola sitting up in a chair reading a book in the middle of the night, the reality of her situation evident by the IV lines spread out neatly over her bed, and the wincing she would make as she moved her failing body. I asked her if she needed anything, and we started to talk. I went to get a chair so I could sit level with her. She talked about her life, her family, her cancer journey, and we chatted for quite a while. Eventually, she told me she was going to die soon, and she had accepted that. I was awe-inspired at not only her acceptance of her own mortality, which is a reality we all face but don't necessarily desire to know when it is coming, but at her ability to talk about it with me. I thought, "how would I behave if I were in her situation? Certainly, not like that. How can she possibly be at such peace?" I was completely amazed at how she handled herself, how she was satisfied with what she had accomplished in her life, and how, in hindsight, she was already living her legacy through me at that very moment.

After speaking for a while, Lola looked down at the book she had been reading, held it out to me and said, "you know what? I want you to have this." At that moment, I thought back to what I was taught about accepting gifts as a professional, and debated internally whether I should take it. I thought, "Is this a gift of value? Should I say no?" When I looked at her at that moment, she answered me without words. Her eyes told me that this was something she needed to do. I knew that whatever the subject, I needed to accept it. I took the book into my hands and ran my fingers over the title. It was a book about the life of Jesus. I thanked her for the conversation and the book and went on to complete my shift.

A few months later, I saw Lola's obituary in the local paper. I read how devoted she was to her life, her family, her church, her career. Her family thanked her caregivers in the obituary, and I wished I could formally thank her the same for what she did for me spiritually on that one night in the hospital. I did not know at the time that as the years passed, I would still look at this moment with such meaning. I like to think she knew that. The true significance of this moment wasn't about the book. It was about the needs of the patient as a person, fulfilling also the needs of the nurse as a person.

My definition of being a professional nurse is to not only conduct oneself to the expectations of the nurse as the employee, but also to embrace the nurse as the legacy. A professional nurse will work every shift beyond the burn-out, beyond the stress, beyond the aggravation, beyond the pain, and employ a spiritual openness when delivering care because one never knows what the nurse walking in the door will experience that will shape a better nurse walking out the door.

I have grown to embrace nursing as a true art, a painting that hangs on the wall long after my time. Each brush stroke I make is another person I have helped, many of whom go on to have families that would not have been possible without the involvement of a nurse. Over time, the brush strokes go on to create a beautiful, unique picture, just like Lola's did. She helped my entire career in twenty minutes.

Because I pulled up a chair.

Spirituality in the nursing workplace is something probably not discussed enough but is such a vital concept in nursing because it is a vital concept to humans. Experientially, nurses tend to avoid engaging in spiritual conversation altogether, fearing it will overlap too closely with religion. Contrarily, spiritually supportive conversation is a major part of therapeutic care delivery and can be neutrally presented. What I learned from my interaction with Lola was that when I allowed her to guide the conversation, it did not lead anywhere she did not want it to go. The result was therapeutic for us both.

Reflection

This small moment of connection between the patient and nurse made a major difference in this author's life. We may not share the same culture or spirituality (inclusive of religion) as our patients, but we as nurses understand that it may be a major component of our patients' lives. Notice how the author never mentions that they shared the same religion as their patient, Lola, but cherished how Lola wanted to share something meaningful with the author. We are privileged to provide solace, comfort, and connection with our patients. An important aspect of nursing is our assessment, and part of this assessment must include a cultural and spiritual assessment so the nurse can best provide resources and support from an informed place. A potential question related to this narrative may be:

A patient recently learned of some difficult news about their prognosis. The nurse enters the patient's room and finds them crying in their bed. After pulling a chair to the side of the bed to sit with the patient, which is the most appropriate question?

- **"May I pray with you?"**
- **"What is making you upset?"**
- **"Is it okay if I sit with you so you can talk about anything you want to?"**
- **"Are you in any pain?"**

Asking the patient if they want to pray is assuming they are religious. The nurse should never assume a patient's religion or spirituality matches the nurse's own. Asking the patient what is making them upset or if they are in any pain are appropriate questions, but don't offer the patient to lead the conversation based on what they just learned. Asking the patient if it is okay to sit with them so they can lead the conversation in a way that is culturally appropriate to them is the most suitable question.

Culture and Spirituality: Competent

Narrative by Peter Stoffan, DNP, MPA, RN, CCRN, NEA-BC, CPXP

One of my most memorable moments as a clinical nurse caring for a patient occurred when I was caring for a patient in the adult surgical step-down unit. The patient had a complex brain tumor that was rapidly progressing and caused an intense number of complications. It seemed that when one thing resolved, ten other things declined. The patient also developed a myriad of infections that required him to be on isolation. This then meant that every task or intervention that needed to occur required planning to ensure the right supplies, medications, tools, and any other materials needed. It ALSO meant that time management was key when taking care of this patient, because it meant that when you entered his room, you would be away from your other patients for a considerable amount of time. But what this also meant was that while you were in the room taking care of him, you would be spending a lot of time with just him. Eventually he was intubated and was unable to communicate…His prognosis was poor, and he had limited or almost no brain activity, and although multiple ethics consults were called to work with the family, the family was adamant that we would continue to take care of him regardless.

This patient eventually received the reputation of being the unwanted assignment on the unit due to the tedious tasks and isolation status. Another consideration was that the family essentially moved in with him in the small New York City corner isolation room…so much so that on multiple occasions, I would enter the room and have to ask the patient's wife (politely) to remove the clothes line full of their own clothes drying that they had washed in the sink because they had not gone home in the past few days due to the potential safety hazards it was causing for them and for the healthcare team.

It was a difficult situation, but I never lost sight of the human behind the diagnosis. I would spend hours in the patient's room each shift and have "discussions" with him (though they were one-way) and ask him how he was doing, and tell him about my day and what I was having for a meal that day, and why I went into Nursing after a career in Musical Theatre. Despite my intention to be human-centered with everything I did, the family would intervene before every IV medication, IV push, turn, bath, lotion…EVERY nursing intervention. The trust between the nurse, patient and/or family was definitely not present.

Eventually through the family, I learned that the patient and his family used to love going to the Philharmonic, especially when the orchestra was celebrating and playing the Strauss Waltzes…so when I was in the room, I would play some classical music for him on my phone while performing my cares, especially Strauss. This changed everything with the relationship. Through showing that I cared about the patient as a human before their prognosis and saw the patient beyond the diagnosis and myriad of countless tasks I needed to accomplish for him every shift, the family trusted me.

After many months of taking care of him through his health decline, I got to know the family well and formed a bond that was meaningful and cemented that we as Nurses are of course clinical experts, but we are also the humans on the other side of the healthcare system for patients and families and communities. Although it was an ethically and emotionally dense situation, it was my duty to care for the patient and family and do everything I could to provide clinical expertise and maintain human dignity. It is our duty to uphold humanhood.

Reflection

There are so many ways to connect with a patient and family and colleagues, it sometimes just requires an open-ended question and time and space for dialogue. It wasn't until the author found that special shared love of music that the nurse-patient-family trusting relationship began to form.

Recognizing culture is an important aspect of care, what is the most appropriate question a nurse can ask a patient's family member to assess a non-verbal patient's culture?

- **What can I do to make their and your experience more comfortable?**
- **What was the patient like before they were in the hospital?**
- **What language does the patient speak?**
- **Do you want me to call Pastoral Care or the Chaplain while you are here?**

While all questions are appropriate and consider aspects of culture and spirituality, the second question may address this most successfully in its open-ended nature. Asking what the patient was like allows the family to share what is most important to them. What makes someone comfortable, someone's language, and spiritual needs are all priorities; we don't know what someone's priority is in terms of their culture and spirituality until we ask them and give space for their specific answer.

Culture and Spirituality: Proficient

Narrative by Molly Jackson, DNP, RN, AGPCNP-C, CNE

When displayed by a nurse, professionalism involves a patient-centered approach that promotes independence and patient autonomy. The nurse serves primarily as an advocate for the patient, who has unique personal, relational, physical, social, and spiritual needs.

In my work as a Palliative Care advanced practice nurse, I primarily cared for patients in their homes suffering from a variety of conditions—from end-stage dementia to chronic obstructive lung disease to cancer. My goal was to assess them and, in collaboration with an interdisciplinary team, help manage bothersome symptoms. Skills such as advanced pain and dyspnea management and conducting goal-directed conversations were foundational. If my patient entered hospice level of care at any point, a different team became involved, and my visits with the patient and family ended.

This narrative centers around a 55-year-old male who I was seeing for supportive management of advanced lung cancer. A former construction worker, he was single and lived alone. His support system was very small, with one sister living nearby who looked after him. She had asked her brother to move in with her, but he declined.

This patient was receiving chemotherapy, but his oncologist had recently informed him that the therapy so far had not been effective in reducing the spread of the cancer. A drain had been inserted into his pleural space to collect fluid that further compressed his lungs and worsened his dyspnea.

We discussed his medical history on my first visit, and I conducted a physical exam. He was cooperative but seemed withdrawn. He reported that his pain was "pretty much" under control, but that he did not like taking opioid medications, as they made him feel woozy. We discussed options to supplement his current pain regime and his advance directives, among other things.

On my next visit with this patient, it seemed that more conversation needed to occur. Though unspoken, we both realized that, between his weight loss, fatigue, and recent oncologist report, the prognosis was poor. He had not expressed his feelings about how this was impacting him, even though I had asked a few open-ended questions to see if he would share his thoughts. I then asked a more direct question: "Sir, if time is short, what is the most important thing to you right now?"

After a long pause, he said, "I don't know if God will forgive me." He then described how he had been involved in service in his church through high school and attended mass regularly. In his early twenties, he became disillusioned by several things and stopped attending church. He recalled a young priest who had supported him in high school, whom he regrettably lost track of, and also said that he wished he was physically strong enough to attend mass again. We discussed God's forgiveness, and a brief prayer was offered with his permission. I noted the priest's name and mentioned to our team the spiritual distress that James was experiencing. His physical condition continued to deteriorate. The patient was admitted to an inpatient hospice facility for more aggressive symptom management and was discharged from our palliative care service.

Two months later, I received a letter addressed to me at my palliative care practice. The patient had died a month before, and his sister was writing. She wrote to express her profound gratitude. Following up on the contact, the hospice team had located the priest, who lived two hours from where my patient was residing. The priest drove to the hospice facility and reconnected with the patient, praying and assuring him of God's love and forgiveness. The sister remarked that this encounter greatly changed his countenance and that he expressed being at peace with himself and with God before his death.

Lessons learned: Realize the impact you can have as a nurse. Don't be afraid to ask questions such as "What is most important (or difficult) for you right now," even if your patients are not in the end stages of illness. Go beyond the pain scale question, and you might be surprised by what your patient will share if you take the time to ask and listen carefully. It can be very therapeutic for a patient to talk about what is on their heart.

Reflection

This reflection highlights the impact we nurses have when we meet our patients where we are and pay attention to the seemingly small or non-clinical pieces of evidence that make a person whole. In this story, the patient revealed to the author something that was weighing on him, and the nurse took it upon herself to connect the patient's priest and patient. This human-centered behavior is what keeps nursing special and unique when compared to all other disciplines and professions. We must consider the entire patient, which means we must also consider the social determinants of health.

Social determinants of health (SDOH) are the non-medical or non-clinical factors that influence one's health, including but not limited to where one lives, grows up, worships, and works (CDC, 2025). Socioeconomic status, or the measure of one's social and economic status within their sphere, impacts one's health: the lower the socioeconomic status, the lower the health (WHO, 2025). Considering one's culture (inclusive of their spirituality or spiritual practices or the absence thereof) is paramount when providing care to patients and families. The absence of considering our patients' full makeup for what makes them "them" does a disservice to our patients and creates a potential for missing key indicators for how we can impact our patients' health and well-being for the better. The author in the above narrative paid attention to her patient's culture and spirituality and intervened at the end of his life to allow a peaceful transition at the end of life.

In lieu of questions related to this narrative, the authors of this publication aim to strengthen your awareness of the social determinants of health as defined by the World Health Organization and the Centers for Disease Control. The authors urge you to review this list and become familiar with SDOH key factors, reflecting on your own SDOH variables and how they vary between you and your colleagues and you and your patient population that you may impact.

SDOH Variables:

- **Safe housing.**
- **Safe transportation.**
- **Safe neighborhoods.**
- **Racism, discrimination, and violence.**
- **Access to education.**
- **Access to job opportunities.**
- **Access to livable income and wages.**
- **Access to nutritious foods.**
- **Access to physical activity opportunities.**
- **Access to clean water and air.**
- **Language and literacy skills.**

References

Center for Disease Control. (2025, March 2). *Social determinants of health*. https://www.cdc.gov/about/priorities/why-is-addressing-sdoh-important.html

World Health Organization. (2025, March 2). *Social determinants of health*. https://www.who.int/health-topics/social-determinants-of-health#tab=tab_1

Culture and Spirituality: Expert

Narrative by Deborah Lindell, DNP, MSN, RN, CNE, ANEF, FAAN

"In many ways the saying, 'know thyself', is not well said. It were more practical to say, "know other people!" Menander, 343–292, Greek poet (in the book *People* by Peter Spier")

I have been a nurse for 56 years and on faculty at a top research institution for about 30 years. Since 2000, I have taught and consulted in Mexico, Vietnam, China, Kenya, and, currently, Hong Kong. I appreciate this opportunity to share an experience about the influence of culture on my life and work.

In April 2021, received a Fulbright Scholar award to implement a project at a small, brand-new public college in remote Turkana County, Kenya. The primary aim of the project was to work with the college to develop a plan for a nursing program. I would live for eight months at a facility owned by a non-governmental organization (NGO). It serves as a base camp for fieldwork, such as fossil hunting, by scientists studying human evolution. I had traveled to the area to visit the college in 2019 during a whirlwind two-night trip to Kenya with a member of the faculty and four grad students. My champion, mentor and Fulbright sponsor was Dr IN, Associate Director of Research for the NGO and one of the visitors to my institution in 2018, when we initiated the partnership. IN was an adjunct member of the faculty at the college and very invested in its success. At the time, he was working with them and raising money to start a new graduate major in evolutionary biology. He aimed to prepare students from Kenya to study evolution in their own country.

During the complex process of preparing for my Fulbright project, including unanticipated surgery, I did not think or ask about the culture. I only knew a few things I learned on my brief trip to Kenya, such as that women in Turkana who wore Western attire dressed conservatively and that I did not "need to learn Swahili" as Kenya is, by law, a dual language country. My time in Kenya was an adventure from day one. I was on my own, living and working with many people I had never met, while trying to implement my project. While Dr IN was supportive, he spent much time in the US and Nairobi; we kept in touch via email and occasional phone calls. I was oriented to the Fulbright program in Sub-Saharan Africa to review policies and some things to expect in the country, including to expect requests for money. I probably envisioned that Miss BO, my staff liaison at the college, would be my champion there but, for complex reasons, that did not turn out to be the case.

As the first several months played out, I realized I was immersed in several new "social groups," each with unique ways of life. If I was to get along and implement my project, I had to try to understand them and learn to function within them. Here are some examples.

Camp: I received no orientation or guidelines at the camp (or at the college for that matter), but realized there was clearly a culture of how things were done. For example, the transportation from the camp in the desert to and from the college was a major cultural reveal. I paid the camp for a driver for the 45-minute drive across the desert to/from the college. After almost missing my ride on the first day and other experiences, I realized I had to schedule the driver a week or so in advance, know where and when to show up, and get to know the drivers well. Also, I was to sit in the front seat, but there would be any number of other riders (staff and local villagers) squeezed into the back seat of the pick-up truck or sitting on benches in the slightly sheltered back of the old but well-maintained Land Rover. It was many months before one of the drivers realized I was paying for each trip.

There was a clear hierarchy at the camp – scientists, grad students, and staff. It seemed I was in the category of scientist, so I lived in a "cottage" rather than the dormitory. A fan and mini fridge were present on my arrival. I later heard I was privileged in that regard even among the scientists. At one time, there had been devices for each cottage, but they were not replaced, so other scientists who were more senior but stayed a few days pre-/post-fieldwork did not have them. On the other hand, I learned to tell when certain senior scientists had arrived because a first course of homemade soup was served and adult beverages appeared. Otherwise, we never had soup and wine except on the occasions when I purchased it in town and shared with the grad students who lived at the camp and with the cook staff.

Another example of hierarchies in the camp was when I arranged a driver to take me to a town two hours away for my research. The assigned vehicle was an old but well-maintained Land Rover with two seats (one driver and one rider) in the cab and benches in the back with a canvas cover. When I got in the Land Rover, I noticed a staff member sitting on the benches. It was only after I almost pleaded with him that he joined myself, and the driver in the front seat. A bit squished but much more comfortable for all.

College: Subtle, or not so, hierarchies were present at the college too. I made two business trips with three colleagues from the college: a Dean, two faculty members, and Miss BO. For the first trip, I rode with the others in a vehicle provided by the college so as to not appear "better than them." As instructed, I had notified the US Embassy about the trip. However, the Embassy didn't see the message until after that trip, when I was clearly informed that I was to fly whenever possible (more on that later). On the 2nd longer trip, I did fly, and the fact that two cars (theirs and my Uber) were trying to arrive at the same location at the same time complicated our trip (they were 30 minutes late). Also, on the way back to Turkana County, the college vehicle was in an accident with severe damage to the car and injuries to my three colleagues, which resulted in a two-month leave of absence for Miss BO. Another observation is that while I stayed in moderately priced hotels, my local colleagues stayed in hostel-type facilities.

In the college, I seemed to have a good working relationship with mid-level faculty and staff while I was there. Several were extremely helpful in helping me prepare for a professional development program I sponsored for area nurses by moving furniture, arranging food and transportation for the nurses, advertising, etc. On the other hand, it seemed communication and decision-making occurred among members of the leadership team (all male) to which I was not privy.

This wasn't helped by the fact that the senior local leader was a different senior leader I had originally met in 2018, prior to arriving to Kenya. This newer senior leader received a limited orientation to the Fulbright program and did not seem invested in my project. Along the way, after I declined to teach the two courses I had been assigned (not part of my project), I ultimately learned that in higher education of countries with emerging economies, having a foreigner on your faculty list was a big deal. I also learned that I would not be developing a new curriculum for the college (part of my proposed project) because the college was not independent of their "mother university" and it was required to use the curricula of that institution, even the syllabi had the name of the mother university printed at the top. I did co-teach two courses (supposed to be 10% per my plan) and wound up doing most of the work because my co-faculty was promptly assigned other responsibilities. I learned a lot about higher education in Kenya, including that grading was reviewed by other internal and external faculty. If I had understood these situations, I might have contacted the Fulbright program and the US Embassy about adjusting my plan. But I didn't, and aspects of the culture at the college made it difficult to implement some aspects of my project.

I hoped to meet with the senior leaders before I left to debrief my experience, but the key person was away around that time, so I couldn't arrange a final meeting. Ultimately, despite submitting an extensive report and recommendations, I had basically no communication with the college after I left Turkana County, and, to my knowledge, there has been no progress on a nursing program. I am happy to report that I did connect with a nursing supervisor from the Ministry of Health and Sanitation to teach at the college, which he has done, and I continue to mentor him.

Societal level: As with the camp and college, through observation and experience, I discovered many aspects of culture in Kenya. Everyone I encountered socially in the Nairobi area and in Turkana County, including villagers, was welcoming and kind. However, there were many hierarchies like those at the camp and college, as well as signs that Kenya continued to reflect being a former colony of Great Britain. The residents of one suburb of Nairobi were middle or upper class and largely white, whereas in Turkana, I was often the only white person I would see for days, whether at college or in town. At camp, everyone was black except foreign scientists and their students.

The language issue was not as straightforward as my Fulbright sponsor indicated. English was prevalent among those I encountered; however, the clear preference was Swahili (or the local dialect in Turkana). Often, I would sit or stand by while people conversed in Swahili, of which I knew just a few words. Also, I learned that while people of Kenya recognized the value of learning English, they resented being required by law to learn the language, as it was seen as a continuation of colonialism. A fun aspect of Kenyan culture is the celebration of birthdays, which I had the opportunity to participate in. I loved how each guest would share something positive about the birthday person. Another tradition was feeding cake. For adults, the birthday person would offer a bite to each guest.

A final example of culture in Kenya was what I would describe as "making the most of a situation or opportunity" but others called bribery or corruption. When my students performed community assessments, they listed the situation of corruption as one of their findings. The reason I was to fly rather than travel by car was that it was not uncommon for bandits on the main road to stop the car and demand money. I was also told police would do the same – you had to pay them on the spot in cash or be taken to local jail for situations like not wearing a mask during the peak of the COVID-19 pandemic. As advised during the Fulbright orientation, I was asked for significant amounts of money – subtlety to support the family of a camp staff member or cornered at a cafe by a college staff member and asked to help with PhD tuition. Lastly, I was going through security at the local airport and had small gifts for nurse leaders I would visit: little pink bags with rose quartz hearts in them and a note about mindfulness attached. After my suitcase was x-rayed, a search ensued, the bags were held up, and I was told it was illegal to take "rocks" out of Kenya. It was obvious these were not ancient artifacts. I explained the pink stones were gifts, polished and shaped as hearts in the US I then asked, "would you like to have one? The response was a smile, an exchange occurred, and my suitcase was cleared.

Lessons Learned and Recommendations

I learned so much during my time in Kenya! First, in writing this narrative, I've learned that the process alone can be a learning experience. I have never been one to keep a journal, but I can now see the value of doing that. For me, writing this narrative has been a time of reflection with a range of emotions and ultimately offering some degree of healing. I couldn't help recalling the extended illness of my college liaison, Miss BO, her car accident and ultimately followed by the unexpected and sudden deaths of both Dr IN and Miss BO within a six-week period. These events, though grief-laden, reinforced my resolve to complete my Fulbright project. Looking back, I now realize that to do so, I had to take on a more assertive and independent leadership role and dug deep into reserves of resilience and persistence I didn't realize I had.

A second takeaway is that culture is everywhere – it is our way of life; how we do things. It is not inherently right or wrong; it just is. Having taught in several countries over the years, I would tell others that while it is important to honor our differences, we should also acknowledge our shared core values and beliefs. This may be true, but having been immersed in at least four different cultures for eight months, I came to realize that our differences are what make us unique – as social groups and as individuals. That is not to say there can't be discussion about how we do things. But let's try not to automatically react that our way is the best way. We can accept there can be different ways to accomplish the same goal or activity. Or, we might even learn that the other's way is better.

I can't emphasize enough the importance of a person-centered lens—in clinical nursing, nursing education, nursing leadership, or for all people. Acknowledge there are unique cultures among individuals, families, work settings, and social groups. Be an observant learner when meeting a new person or going into a new setting. If appropriate, ask for an orientation. Be respectful and curious – "tell me about your daily life, how do you do XXX?" Culture is embedded; for individuals, it meshes with one's personality, and in social settings, it meshes with structures like rules and policies.

For example, doing this reflection has led me to realize, and work on accepting, that each of my adult children have developed unique cultures within their homes and families that are different from how they grew up. Call them ways of life, preferences, or rules, but they are there, and my husband and I need to accept and honor them.

Reflection

This author reveals that culture is all around us, in the school, the camp, and in the ways we are immersed in the societies we find ourselves. Dr Lindell reflects on culture in the camp, college, and in the overall local Kenyan society she was immersed in for eight months. The story she tells about the hired driver and how this may have been perceived by the other camp scientists, workers, and locals reveals a vast difference in culture and expectations. And the second story about the staff member sitting in the back of the Land Rover, solely based on the hierarchy of the camp politics, reveals a culture that had been set well before Dr Lindell arrived in Kenya. Why should someone sit in the back of the truck when there is room up front? Well, the culture had dictated it to be the practice...Do we ever prepare for cultural differences and perform due diligence before we are faced with the cultural realities, or do we just assume that we are all alike until we quickly realize this is not the case? Same for our patients, families, communities, and colleagues – do we research prior to jumping in? Dr Lindell mentioned asking questions and touched upon the aspect of curiosity for differences before assuming similarities.

The Western expectations regarding travel and lodging are revealing of the cultural differences in this narrative. Dr Lindell also touches upon how, while some local colleagues were helpful in her mission to improve education for nurses in Kenya, she, as a woman, had fewer privileges and less information than her male colleagues. Once again, this reflection reveals the difference between expectations and reality in relation to culture. This narrative mentions that there is a stark racial divide in Kenya because of the history of British colonialism, which highlights that history is informative, not always right, but it is there. Understanding a location's and a person's history is part of understanding their culture. Without this understanding, one won't ever fully understand the culture of that individual or community.

There is a South African Zulu tribal saying, "ubuntu," that, when loosely translated, means "I am because you are" or "until I see you, I do not exist." This cultural saying encapsulates the curiosity, understanding, and acceptance of another's culture, inclusive of their spirituality, necessary for a successful human existence. Ask yourself, do you live by this thought? Do you seek to understand and accept others before you move through your existence as a nurse, leader, friend, partner, teacher, or family member? How can you start incorporating this practice into your daily life?

Instead of potential NCLEX-RN questions after this narrative, the authors want to urge you, the reader, to consider potential ways you can explore international opportunities for professional development in your nursing career.

Chapter 6

Nursing Process: Introduction

We as nurses rely on our intellect to appropriately and safely care for our patients, families, and communities. Ultimately, the way we manage the care of others is rooted in the nursing process (ANA, 2025). ADPIE is an acronym used for the five components of the nursing process. ADPIE stands for: Assessment, diagnosis, planning, implementation and evaluation (see Figure 6.1).

The schematic of this process represents the continuum or constant process that the nurse utilizes through the ever-changing conditions of our patients. One assessment or one diagnosis to plan one intervention with one evaluation is never enough for our patients, as humans are constantly changing. This process is similar to the quality improvement Plan, Do, Study, Act or PDSA cycle. The PDSA cycle, originated by Edward Deming in 1986 and later adopted in healthcare, is an iterative way to evaluate improvements and must be repeatedly refined for the best outcomes

 DOI: 10.4324/9781003586548-6

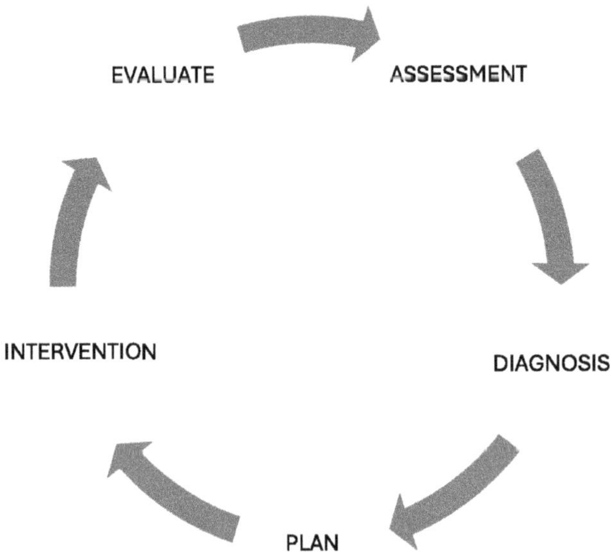

Figure 6.1 Components of the Nursing Process: ADPIE.

(Taylor et al, 2014). If we view the nursing process through a similar lens as a constant and repeated cycle of care, our patients will benefit.

This chapter contains narratives, reflections, and questions that urge you, the reader, to consider how the characters in the narratives utilize the nursing process to drive outcomes. The nursing process is not solely used as objectively clinical as you will read. The nursing process may be used to consider an environment or workflows, in addition to individuals' disease processes. The nursing process is a foundational framework that can be applied to all situations by professional nurses, no matter the role. As a clinical nurse, the nursing process can help identify the best route forward for a patient care plan. As a nurse educator, the nursing process can guide the efficacy of a lesson plan. As a nurse leader, the nursing process can help identify strategic plans for teams and systems. As you read the narratives, reflections, and questions, consider how you can utilize the nursing process to guide your actions both in and outside the nursing and healthcare realm.

References

American Nurses Association. (2025, April 26). *The nursing process.* https://www.nursingworld.org/practice-policy/workforce/what-is-nursing/the-nursing-process/

Taylor, M. J., McNicholas, C., Nicolay, C., Darzi, A., Bell, D., & Reed, J. E. (2014). Systematic review of the application of the plan-do-study-act method to improve quality in healthcare. *BMJ Quality & Safety*, 23(4): 290–298. https://doi.org/10.1136/bmjqs-2013-001862

Nursing Process Narrative: Novice

Narrative by Katelynn Dharap, MBA, MSN, RN, NEA-BC

When I was eight years old, I was diagnosed with Immune Thrombocytopenia Purpura (ITP), leading to years of treatment at my local children's hospital on the hematology/oncology unit. The healthcare professionals, especially the nurses, left an impression on me. This inspired me to become a nurse myself, with a dream of caring for pediatric hematology/oncology patients.

Years later, I finally had an interview with the nurse manager of the same unit where I had been a patient. Although I didn't plan to mention my past as a patient, she recognized my name. The interview was going well until she expressed a concern: "I will hire you because I think you are the right fit for the position, but I am concerned that you have ITP." She explained that I would not be allowed to share my patient history with any patients or their families, as oncologic patients have different treatments and experiences from hematologic patients. Despite finding this interaction unusual, I accepted the job.

Soon, my former nurses became my coworkers. They were thrilled to see a former patient thriving and inspired to become a nurse because of them. However, they couldn't understand why I was prohibited from sharing my ITP experience with patients. I, too, was puzzled but didn't want to jeopardize my dream job. My coworkers were eager to learn from my firsthand experience, which enriched their understanding of caring for the patient with ITP.

One day, I was assigned to a 14-year-old patient that verbalized her struggle with the new ITP diagnosis. She felt isolated and longed to be anywhere but the hospital. Other nurses avoided her due to her complex treatment and family dynamics. This patient reminded me of myself at her age, so I decided to break the rules and share my own ITP experience with her. I explained that while every patient's journey is unique, I understood her feelings of isolation and wanted her to know she wasn't alone. This revelation transformed this patient's outlook. Her attitude improved, and her family trusted my clinical judgment, asking questions they might not have asked others; she looked forward to my shifts and the time we spent together.

While my boss might have deemed my actions unprofessional, I believe that honesty and connection are crucial for effective patient care. Human connection is vital in the art of nursing. A few years later, a nurse who had survived cancer as a child was hired, and his story was celebrated in a press release. This made me realize that the nurse manager's restriction was specific to my ITP diagnosis. Had it been cancer, my story would have been widely shared. I often wonder how many more patients I could have connected with if I had been allowed to share my experience. Restrictions on sharing firsthand experiences can limit the potential for connection and understanding between healthcare providers and patients. It's important to evaluate the reasons behind such restrictions and consider their impact on patient care.

Reflection

In the case of this patient, this author used the nursing process and assessed the patient and ultimately understood that sharing a personal story would help improve the patient's outlook. The author understood the patient's diagnosis and planned the care for this patient accordingly. Not all patients or situations are the same; therefore, this author did not listen to the nurse manager's (poor) guidance to withhold but instead leaned into the human connection to build a nurse/patient trusting relationship that would ultimately benefit the patient to flourish, similarly to how the author did.

When considering the nursing process, we may immediately think about how we can use the ADPIE (Assessment, Diagnosis, Planning/Outcome, Implementation, Evaluation) model in a clinical way. This author used the nursing process from beginning to end in a psychosocial manner. The author assessed the patient and understood that a unique tactic would have to be employed to foster a trusting relationship. Because the author knew personally what an ITP diagnosis would mean, the author could plan patient-centered education and empowerment that could immediately be implemented. Eventually, the author was able to evaluate the success of the trusting relationship through verbal feedback from the patient and family and was able to continue the nursing process cycle, beginning with assessing the patient's and family's needs at every new shift.

A potential question related to this scenario is:

A nurse is reviewing a care plan and discharge education with a client with thrombocytopenia. The nurse understands that education has been successful if the client repeats the following:

- **"I should only shave once a week."**
- **"I should use a soft-bristled toothbrush when brushing my teeth."**
- **"It is okay for me to take aspirin, but not ibuprofen."**
- **"I can resume taking my daily supplements, including Ginkgo."**

The nurse uses the nursing process to assess if the education was understood in this scenario. Patients with thrombocytopenia can shave when needed or wanted but should use an electric razor to reduce bleeding risk. Aspirin and all non-steroidal anti-inflammatory drugs, such as ibuprofen, should be avoided. The patient should ask the provider which medications can be taken as needed for minor aches. Supplements should be examined before taking, and it should be communicated that supplements such as ginkgo biloba, garlic, ginger, ginseng, and others can be natural anti-inflammatory agents. Patients with thrombocytopenia should use soft-bristled toothbrushes; therefore, this statement triggers the nurse to evaluate that the education was successful.

Nursing Process Narrative: Beginner

Narrative by Emily Hanna, BSN, RN-BC, CCRN

I have dedicated nearly a decade to patient care, initially on an Electrophysiology Step-Down Unit, followed by critical care roles in the Float Pool and Cardiovascular Intensive Care Unit (CVICU). Throughout my career, I have gained invaluable experience in managing complex cases, such as heart and lung transplants and patients requiring life-saving devices like Extracorporeal Membrane Oxygenation (ECMO) and Ventricular Assist Devices (VADs).

One of the most profound experiences that required my leadership and professionalism occurred while working in the CVICU. I was the primary nurse for a heart transplant patient who, despite initially thriving post-surgery, faced a devastating setback six months later. Upon readmission, his condition deteriorated rapidly, and he required ECMO to sustain his failing heart. Over the course of his prolonged hospitalization, I became deeply involved in both his care and his family's journey, navigating the challenges of ECMO while also serving as their emotional anchor. Recognizing the limitations of our medical interventions, I used my clinical knowledge and leadership skills to advocate for the patient's wishes as his condition worsened. At one point, the medical team considered discontinuing ECMO, believing further treatment would be futile. However, the patient had expressed a strong desire to return home before passing, and I felt a deep responsibility to honor his wishes. I led conversations with the care team, ensuring his autonomy was respected and that every possible effort was made to fulfill his final goal. While he ultimately couldn't be discharged, we managed to stabilize him without ECMO for several days, giving him and his family cherished moments of closure.

This experience taught me several invaluable lessons about leadership and professionalism in nursing. First, advocacy is essential—patients and their families rely on us not just for our clinical expertise but for our ability to stand up for their wishes and rights. Second, leadership in nursing is not always about making decisions; it's often about facilitating discussions and ensuring that the patient's voice is heard amid the complexities of medical treatment. Third, empathy and emotional intelligence are as crucial as technical skills, especially when dealing with end-of-life situations. Lastly, I learned that while we cannot always control outcomes, we can control the quality of care we provide. Creating an environment where patients feel heard and their dignity is preserved is one of the most important aspects of our role as healthcare professionals.

For those beginning or continuing their journey in healthcare, I offer the following recommendations: always be an advocate, remembering that patients may not have the knowledge or strength to speak for themselves. Step into that role, even when it's uncomfortable or challenging. Embrace empathy—leadership in nursing is not just about managing care; it's about managing people. Cultivating empathy and understanding can significantly impact patient outcomes and team dynamics. Be open to learning, as every situation, especially the difficult ones, provides an opportunity to grow. Reflect on both your successes and failures, and always strive to improve. Lastly, honor patient wishes. At the heart of professionalism is respect for patient autonomy. In complex cases, their desires should be central to the care plan, even when their condition makes this difficult. By integrating these principles into your practice, you will not only provide excellent care but also lead by example, inspiring others to do the same.

Reflection

This author relied on the nursing process in many aspects of the care she provided. First, the author assessed the patient and understood the diagnosis and clinical considerations for a heart transplant patient. The author created a nursing plan that considered the heart failure and understood that the plan would be a psychosocial-focused nursing plan due to the clinical futility of the patient's situation. The author shifted focus to advocacy and empathy for the patient and family. The nurse assessed the overall situation, diagnosed the patient as dying, planned to advocate for the patient to be as comfortable as possible, and implemented this plan through leading discussions with her interprofessional team members. Though the patient was unable to have his wish be granted to die in the comfort of his home surrounded by loved ones, the nurse was able to ensure a secure and comforting transition to death as possible and ultimately evaluated that she did as much as she could while protecting the safety and well-being of her patient.

Once again, we see the nursing process being played out in an overarching, all-encompassing way. We may not "feel" the nursing process the same way we would when first approaching a newly diagnosed patient or in a straightforward case study, but the nursing process is employed regardless. Relying on the nursing process as a healing force in a patient's and family's and community's sphere is our calling as nurses.

A potential question related to this scenario is:

The nurse understands that ECMO is not indicated for the following patient:

- **A patient with advanced lung disease who has been denied a lung transplant.**

- **A patient awaiting a heart transplant.**
- **A pediatric patient with persistent pulmonary hypertension.**
- **A patient undergoing a cardiac catheterization procedure**.

All of the above patients may be candidates for ECMO except the patient with advanced lung disease, who has been denied a lung transplant. ECMO should not be used as a fail-safe or a long-term option. The nurse should understand that for this patient, an ethics consult should be called and an interprofessional team meeting, including the patient and family, should consider options and make a care plan for this advanced patient.

Nursing Process Narrative: Competent

Narrative by Akeliah Robertson, BSN, RN, CCRN

I am a Coronary ICU nurse with a background in med-surg and medical intensive care unit (MICU) nursing. My journey as a nurse started in South Florida and exposed me to diverse populations. With that comes unique challenges and opportunities for growth. This has allowed me to see how empathy and professionalism in patient care go a long way in helping patients and family members feel safe and supported.

During one of my shifts in the MICU, I cared for a male patient in his 60s who had been intubated for a few days. We had started to wean sedation so we could prepare to extubate him. During the report, I was told he was restrained due to previous attempts to remove his tube. When I assessed him at the start of my shift, I found him completely alert, oriented and assessed him for delirium using the Confusion Assessment Method (CAM), and he was CAM-negative (meaning not delirious). I then decided that I would try to figure out why he was attempting to remove the tube since he was aware of his situation and what initially led to him being intubated.

I started by asking him simple yes-or-no questions to see why he was agitated overnight. After about 30 minutes of conversation, using my judgment, I decided that if he could safely communicate, removing his restraints would prevent him from trying to remove the tube. He wanted to write, so I handed him a marker and a paper. He thanked me profusely and explained that the tube during the night was his main reason for being upset. I assured him that I would speak with the doctors to find out when the tube could be removed since he was breathing on his own and completely alert.

He wrote on the paper that he wanted to speak with his daughter. Although he couldn't talk, I relayed messages between them by changing her questions to a yes-or-no format. The moment he made a heart sign with his hands, I asked for permission to take a photo to send to his daughter. She was so happy she started to cry.

Later, when the family visited, his daughter hugged me and thanked me for making her feel comfortable and for reassuring her that her dad was safe and being well taken care of. The next day, after he was extubated, we spent a lot of my shift talking about his life before he was in the hospital. Both he and his daughter repeatedly thanked me for the care that I was giving and the picture I had sent.

In nursing, there are times when decisions must be made, and you will be unsure of how it will turn out. I often think back to a quote. I'm not sure if I heard it in a movie or saw it on social media. It said: "What if everything goes wrong? But what if everything goes right?" It is such a simple quote, but over the years I've often found myself going back to it when faced with decisions, not only in patient care but in my life. This quote was what guided my actions during this situation. I looked at it from both ways: What if he removed the tube? What if it led to re-intubation? But then I looked from the other end: What if removing the restraints allowed him to feel more in control? What if he could finally change the channels on the TV on his own? What if he could do the crossword puzzle his family left him? What if removing the restraints made him feel safe?

In this case, everything went right. He was able to communicate through writing, and we were better able to address his needs. Looking back on this moment always reminds me that there is such a fine line us nurses walk on as we balance risk and reward. As nurses, we can acknowledge risks but also see the potential for positive outcomes when we lead with empathy.

This experience helped me to trust my nursing judgment more and showed me that it is okay to sometimes take risks when they align with what the patient truly needs. While

I naturally tend to play it safe, my memories of situations like this remind me to be okay with opportunities to create meaningful change, even when I'm faced with a difficult decision.

Reflection

This author relied on the nursing process to assess the patient (using a validated tool – the CAM) for delirium, diagnosing the patient as alert and oriented and non-delirious, planning an intervention, and evaluating the efficacy of allowing the patient to communicate by removing unnecessary wrist restraints. This patient-centered initiative immediately changed the clinical course for this patient; by removing the wrist restraints, the patient was able to successfully communicate with the clinical team and his loved ones. Relying on the nursing process in this specific situation reversed the unnecessary restraining of a patient and potentially reduced ventilator hours and sedation and therefore improved this patient outcome. NOTE: at times, physical restraints may be necessary to protect patients and reduce harm (patient and clinical team harm), but should be used as a last resort with a provider's order, and in conjunction with constant nursing assessments and reassessments for utility.

A potential question related to this scenario may be:

A patient has been recently admitted to the medical intensive care unit. The patient is mildly sedated, intubated with an endotracheal (ET) tube. Due to combative behavior immediately upon admission, the provider writes an order for two-point wrist restraints. The nurse understands that part of the assessment for this patient must include the following: (Select all that apply)

- **Patient comfort.**
- **Skin integrity.**
- **Range of motion.**
- **Delirium.**

When a patient is placed on restraints, constant assessments and reassessments should occur. Additionally, freeing patients and providing restraint breaks every two hours (at least) is necessary. The nurse must also assess the patient's skin integrity and range of motion regularly. Other regular assessments must include the patient's circulation to ensure the restraints are not prohibiting adequate blood flow. Delirium should be assessed regularly to be able to wean the patient off the intubation and restraints. While a patient is in restraints, the nurse must also consider the patient's comfort and basic needs, such as hydration and toileting. Therefore, all options are appropriate assessments.

References

Wei, L. A., Fearing, M. A., Sternberg, E. J., & Inouye, S. K. (2008). The Confusion Assessment Method: a systematic review of current usage. Journal of the American Geriatrics Society, 56(5), 823–830. https://doi.org/10.1111/j.1532-5415.2008.01674.x

Nursing Process Narrative: Proficient

Narrative by Mary Joy Garcia-Dia, DNP, RN, FAAN, FHIMSS

I started my career in nursing in New York in 1988 at an academic medical center after being recruited from the Philippines during the height of the AIDS (acquired immunodeficiency syndrome) epidemic. Due to the nursing shortage, I quickly became a charge nurse right after I completed my one-month orientation in a 36-bed medical-surgical unit. A year later, our head nurse went into maternity leave, and as the most senior staff, I stepped in to assume the charge nurse role almost daily, as newer internationally educated nurses were being oriented together with fresh graduates from nursing schools.

During the 1980s, functional nursing was used as a labor assignment model due to the shortage of professional registered nurses. In this care model, the nurse only works on the tasks assigned by the head nurse or supervisor. For each shift, anyone can be assigned as the charge nurse, responsible for taking care of the entire unit while managing staff's activities or responding to concerns brought to by any care team members (Staff nurses, Attending Physician, Resident, Medical Student, Nutritionist or Social Worker). One of the responsibilities of the charge nurse is to pick up orders – this means that all non-medication orders are manually transcribed on the Kardex, while medication orders are re-written on the paper medication administration record. Although there is a unit clerk that assists, the charge nurse needs to review, sign off and cross-check the transcribed orders. Miscommunication can happen, especially for medications, as another staff nurse is responsible for giving out the medications for the entire unit.

The assigned medication nurse waits for the pharmacy to switch the medication bins. Except for narcotics, each bin contains the medications for the patients for the entire 24 hours. The medication nurse covers approximately half a mile of walking while pushing the medication cart from Bed 1 to Bed 36, which is at the end of the hallway. Depending on the patient's condition, the "medication nurse" is often interrupted to give STAT medications, do skin-test (PPD or allergy testing) or give intramuscular/oral medications for pain, fever or vomiting as needed on top of passing out scheduled oral medications, preparing intravenous medications, checking vital signs for cardiac medications. I recall feeling stressed when I am assigned to do medications. I often miss my break or skip lunch to avoid delays in passing time-sensitive medications like antibiotics or STAT medications. I did not have the time to talk to my patients as I needed to move to the next room to finish passing out the medications on time. Whenever the doctor or social worker asks a question about the patient that is not related to medications, I would tell them to look in the chart, feeling frustrated and inadequate. Compared to how I was trained during my nursing school days, I was familiar with the patient's history, chief complaints, medications, and disposition. Aside from passing the medications, the "medication nurse" is responsible for the narcotic count. This is done manually at the start and at the end of every shift to check for any narcotic discrepancy. This is a huge responsibility as nobody can leave work until the narcotic count is completed.

Our medical-surgical unit took care of the homeless population, and there was a high number of intravenous drug users, increasing the risk of exposure to HIV infection. Morale and engagement are low among our team. The work environment was hostile as people felt the burden of caring for HIV patients while feeling vulnerable that they can be infected with a needle prick. Our newer nurses were intimidated and did not feel confident in escalating clinical issues to the medical team. Our nursing assistants, with 10–15 years' experience, were burned out as they do the same mundane tasks daily. Compared to other medical-surgical units, our unit, located on the 16th Floor West area, is labeled as "16**W**orst."

When I stepped into the leadership role as the temporary "head nurse" daily, I knew I needed to change the workload assignment and improve how we work together as a team. I leaned in on my clinical training from the Philippines and introduced the idea of primary care/team-based nursing models. I created three teams to manage our 36-bed capacity medical-surgical unit. Each team is comprised of three staff members (registered nurse (RN), licensed practical nurse (LPN), and a nursing assistant) who are responsible in managing a group of 12 patients. In addition to shift-to-shift handoff, I introduced the process of facilitating a case study discussion, motivating staff to learn about the patient's pathophysiology and treatment plan. We spend 15–30 minutes at the start of each shift reviewing patients' history, chief complaints, and plan of care. This mini huddle sets the tone on what the entire day would look like. Everyone is aware of what the priorities are (from discharges, procedures, referrals) and coordinates these activities to minimize delays. The primary RN are the team leaders and conduct bedside rounds with the medical providers, sharing clinical observations, patients' status, and complaints. As a result, nurses share the information and plan of care in a timely manner with the social worker, nutritionist, respiratory therapist, or patient advocate. The nurses became more attuned on why the medications were ordered for the patient as they had the opportunity to clarify during rounds. Through these interactions, the medical team can revise or enter a new order close to real time, minimizing the back-and-forth paging and telephone tags. The nursing assistants work with their team members in following up specimen collection, dressing changes, frequent rounding and assisting patients with toileting needs. The charge nurse provides support and assists in escalating and resolving issues in real time while occasionally stepping in to take care of patients as needed.

After three months, our staff's attitude changed from being adversarial to more collaborative in nature. Through teamwork, holistic approach, and interprofessional engagement, staff expressed that they know their patients better and engaged with the providers with confidence. The doctors responded timely when they are paged and talked to the nurses directly, as they started to know the nurses' names versus just asking who the medication nurse is. Before, they simply entered an order without communicating their assessment or findings and just flagged the chart for new orders. When we are in the middle of our nursing case discussions, the medical team would wait for our team or would knock on the glass door to respectfully ask if we are ready to go rounding with them. The social worker engaged with the charge nurse daily, identifying patients waiting for discharge, thus reducing wait times for those that may need bed placement in the homeless shelters. The medical team started requesting from the bed board team to admit their patients to 16West. The clinical instructor who follows up students was pleased that the nursing students can shadow staff effectively and did not feel intimidated either. These interprofessional collaboration was not noticeable from my end until one day, Dr Mackey, an attending physician, was walking on the hallway, approached me, and said, "This unit has really changed from **16Wors**t to "**16Wonderful!"** Other medical-surgical nursing units noted the change and eventually adopted primary care/team-based nursing. I was promoted to the head nurse position after one year, and it was heartwarming that our Director of Nursing, Ms Anne MacDonald, and Supervisor, Ms Wilhelmina Gooden, gave me a bulletin board that has the words "From Worst to Wonderful."

My Filipino heritage profoundly shaped my leadership style and professional outlook. The values of bayanihan (community collaboration), kapwa (profound empathy), and matatag (resilience) guided my work. Growing up in a culture that values resourcefulness and adaptability has helped me approach challenges creatively, finding solutions even in resource-constrained environments. The spirit of bayanihan reminds me that the best solutions come from working collectively, valuing every voice in the room, and emphasizing that real solutions arise when diverse voices come together. My heritage has also taught me to approach challenges with kapwa, ensuring that people—not just processes or technology—remain central to decision-making. Resilience (matatag), a hallmark of Filipino culture, has empowered me to lead with courage and adaptability, even in the face of complex systemic barriers. My cultural foundation continually reminds me to lead inclusively, fostering trust and connection within the interprofessional healthcare team.

Reflecting on every epidemic that affected people's lives, from AIDS, Ebola outbreak, and the recent COVID-19 tragedy, our foundational training as nurses equipped us to navigate and lead with courage and compassion. In my current role as program director in nursing informatics, my clinical background imparted in me a unique and valuable perspective in creating inclusive, human-centered solutions by keeping people – patients, clinicians, and communities—at the heart of every innovation. Be fearless in advocating for changes that prioritize usability, equity, and access. Leadership is not about titles; it is about the courage to drive transformation and the humility to learn along the way. Remember that your compassion, resilience, and cultural heritage are not just strengths, they are the foundation of your ability to lead with authenticity and purpose. Step forward with confidence and know that your work will inspire others while shaping a more inclusive, human-centered future for healthcare. Above all, stay true to your purpose – your resilience, empathy, and adaptability make you a leader who can transform not just systems, but people's lives, around the world.

Reflection

This accomplished author highlights how the nursing process can be used as a framework for changing the nursing practice environment. The author fully reshaped and effectively revitalized a unit that was failing its workers and patients. Through assessing what needed to change, diagnosing the workflow problem, planning a desirable outcome to achieve, implementing the new workflow and roles, and ultimately evaluating its success, this narrative perfectly highlights how nurses are leaders and, through the nursing process framework, positive outcomes can be accomplished.

A potential question related to this scenario is:

> **The primary nurse caring for a client newly diagnosed with HIV understands that the client may benefit from the following (select all that apply):**
>
> - **Community resources for support groups.**
> - **Education focused on communication with sexual partners.**
> - **Review of the injection schedule for cabotegravir/rilpivirine.**
> - **Scheduled follow-up appointments.**

The primary nurse assesses the needs of this patient and understands that all of the options are necessary for this patient. Someone newly diagnosed may need additional community support resources, education focused on how to disclose HIV status and the importance of doing so with sexual partners, a review of the injection schedule for cabotegravir/rilpivirine (every two months) if this is the prescribed medication for this patient, and would benefit from routinely scheduled follow-up appointments with the nurse and associated clinic.

Nursing Process Narrative: Expert

Narrative by Angela Prestia, PhD, RN, NE-BC, FAAN

It is September 2004 in Florida. Peak hurricane season. The east coast of Florida, specifically Jupiter, Florida, was anticipating a direct hit from Hurricane Jean. It was expected to make landfall as a category three (3) storm with winds between 111–129 miles per hour.

As a Floridian since age 15, I am no stranger to hurricanes. However, this time it was different. You see, I was in my first year of my first Chief Nursing Officer (CNO) role at a 200-bed not-for-profit medical center. The medical center did not belong to a "system." There was no overarching chief nurse from which to seek advice. I was responsible for the protection and well-being of the patients and staff. Fortunately, I was working in tandem with a supportive Chief Executive Officer (CEO), Safety Officer, and Facilities Director, although he was the only other experienced storm trooper. Additional context requires me to share that at the time, I was a single mother of two children. My son was away at college in Kentucky. My daughter was in college, coming home due to the university closing. I was also a homeowner with no one but the two of us to put up shutters and prepare the house for any ensuing mayhem.

As CNO, my initial responsibilities during the hurricane watch were to collaborate with the physicians and case managers to determine which patients were stable enough to be discharged home. Nursing and pharmacy personnel coordinated care so that medications, including oxygen, could be obtained. Any obstetrical patient 38 weeks plus and a significant other were able to shelter at the hospital. Unless in active labor, they would care for themselves. I also participated in the decision-making regarding those needing acute admission and the cessation of surgery. This tapering off of operations helped determine number of staff truly needed to care for the remaining patients.

Although this responsibility was new to me, I was not afraid. At the time, I did not realize that I was tapping into my inner strength, my courage to continue to lead through this complexity and chaos. I was also operationalizing the Covenant.[1] This is the unspoken promise nurse leaders embrace to "emotionally invest in human caring, fully engage in all role responsibilities, work to co-create a culture of caring, be authentically present with every interaction, and genuinely commit to collaborate to achieve quality patient outcomes" (Prestia, 2023 p. 16).

As the hurricane watches turned into warnings, the medical center's leadership activated the disaster plan. This allowed me an opportunity to secure my home just prior to the beginning of the "during" phase. I would be on duty in the hospital not just for the duration of the storm, but until the roads were passable, and a nursing supervisor could relieve me. My daughter would come with me and shelter in my office.

Upon my return to the medical center, my primary role function became that of "bed placement coordinator." I was assigning beds/rooms to staff who would work and sleep in shifts. This was a pencil and paper clipboard exercise, as there was no electronic capability to manage this. As I continually rounded in sneakers and scrubs, I was challenged by the ever-changing information I was receiving. I had one young nurse approach me in tears, saying she could no longer stay at work, as her horses needed to be sheltered. Dilated pupils told the tale of her fear as she turned and walked off the job.

Tangential to this story, but extremely significant, is the large numbers of elderly volunteer-based auxiliary on record. The majority of this volunteer base consisted of seniors who are affectionately nicknamed snowbirds, as they winter in Florida and return home in the spring. These auxilians have donated their time, treasures, and talents, generating millions of dollars for the benefit of the organization. They expected, no demanded to be sheltered at the organization. If not, a respectable number would return to empty homes.

Pressured by the Director of the Foundation, a very hesitant volunteer Auxilian President paid me a visit. He was seeking a solution, admitting he was at a loss as to what to do with these adamant volunteers. He had received numerous phone calls from their "up-north" family members echoing the need to provide them with shelter. Although minimizing the number of souls in the building made rational sense, we worked through this fluid list together, relieved when someone found other, perhaps safer accommodations.

As the storm's intensity grew, the windows began to shake. The CEO radioed me to the command center. He told me that there were not enough shutters to cover the windows of all five (5) floors. The task then became not only to condense patients and staff horizontally, but also vertically. We closed floors four and five and moved patients into the hallways to avoid the potential consequences of shattering glass. I lead by example, assisting in transferring patients between floors and into the hallways. Privacy was mindfully managed.

Methodic in my rounding, I found my way into the emergency department. This was the last open door as the engineers had shuttered all other entrances. I stepped outside to view the vertically falling rain and could feel the wind intensifying around me. As I took a deep breath of my last bit of fresh air, there was a blast of lightning as the main generator blew right before our eyes. It took a minute for the backup generator to come on. The resulting illumination was minimal. Only critical areas had power, and the majority of the medical center was cast into darkness.

Simultaneously, we received word that the winds had exceeded fifty (50) miles per hour. The ambulances would now stop transporting patients. As I turned to make my way back to the command center, one stray ambulance pulled into our bay area. The snippet of report I received was of a 60 + year-old semi-conscious, inebriated male, who had crashed his golf cart. He needed our care. He had no identification on his person. The remarks about this fellow's drunken joy ride spread like wildfire. Staff shook their heads as they contemplated the "foolish behavior."

Back in the command center, I helped to brainstorm why the backup generators were not working to their fullest capacity. This issue became critical as we received via walkie-talkie that the CAT scanner would not power up. It was not getting the "juice" it needed to work properly. Our patient in the ED needed his abdomen scanned. His expanding girth was cause for concern. Fortunately, the operating suite had emergency power. A general surgeon and an obstetrician/gynecologist performed an exploratory laparotomy. The medical team was able to stop the bleeding, and the patient was stable for now.

During this time, a baby was born via flashlight and basic healthcare ingenuity. A tree crashed into a window with minimal damage. The roof leaked; the toilets would not flush, the phone lines and cell phone towers were down. As I continued my rounds, staff were genuinely happy, projecting a sleep-away camp kind of vibe. The remaining patients, staff, and volunteers settled in for the night. I was thankfully relieved by a rested night shift supervisor who told me, "Hey, I got this!" I returned to my office, exhausted but exhilarated. For now, all is well. My daughter and I fell asleep side by side, holding hands, silent prayers on our lips.

And then – guess what happened next? The sun rose, and the shifts changed. The head of the dietary department was able to prepare the most delicious scrambled eggs you have ever tasted with a steaming cup of coffee. As Star Trek Captain Kirk would say, "Damage control report," – lots of buckets, lots of water encroaching the corridors, but no slips, trips, or falls. No patient, staff, or volunteer injuries. Everyone was safe. Now we wait to see if staff can make it in from their homes for the "after party!"

Oh yes, and one more detail…You know that inebriated patient that everyone was judging? Well, he was actually a "hero." Having secured his home, he decided to have a cocktail or two and wait out the storm. Just as he was getting comfortable, an SOS came from his neighbor; could he spare a jug of gasoline to run a generator? Being the kind, generous person he was, he set off in his golf cart, delivered the gasoline, and on the return home, blinded by the rain, hit something he could not see, upending his golf cart.

I believe that the fabric of our lives and careers is remembered as we recount and retell our stories. When I think about the "moral" of my shared story, well Aesop fans, there are several.

1. Be courageous. You have an incredible well of strength. Care enough as a nurse leader to tap into it.
2. Remember the Covenant. Nursing leadership requires you to consciously care for those you serve.
3. Self-care is critical. Fill up your cup first, and you will be better able to care for others.
4. Build relationships. Nurture them. Acknowledge the role they play in your life.
5. Do not judge a book by its cover. Every one of us has a right to quality healthcare.
6. Review, debrief, and reflect with each situational opportunity. This helps us to grow and develop as nurse leaders.
7. Gain perspective. Change for the better.

Reflection

This author recounts an important story here, highlighting how she used the nursing process during a harrowing time in her career. She had to immediately assess the situation and threats to her patients and teams, diagnose the impact of what was coming their way, plan for the worst event she had seen in her leadership career, implement an emergency response, and constantly evaluate her choices and the outcomes for the patients and team members in her care. Although there may not be an NCLEX-RN-specific question for this scenario, the authors of this book urge you to consider the environmental and climate change-related possibilities that exist in your sphere, wherever you may be reading. Where we choose to work and provide care has its own specific challenges, whether you are in monsoon or typhoon territory, or an area where tornadoes and power outages occur, or hurricanes or heat and/or cold fronts are regular occurrences. No matter where, the external environment impacts how we provide care and how we need to be prepared to adjust our nursing process to benefit ourselves, our patients and families, and our communities.

Reference

Prestia, A.S. (2023) Becoming the CNO: The Science, The Stories, The Truth. ISBN #979-8- 218-35301-8

Chapter 7

Teaching and Learning: Introduction

Nursing is a teaching-learning process. Throughout their work with clients, families, and colleagues, nurses are both constantly learning and constantly teaching.

In every encounter and in every nurse-patient relationship, there is evidence of teaching. And there are many modalities that nurses use in the teaching-learning encounters with their patients. Nurses engage in formal and informal teaching in every encounter with patients. And, importantly, the nurses' own healthy behaviors serve as a teaching moment for modeling health for others. Teaching through modeling the way, serving as a role model of health and healthy behaviors to patients, families, and clinical colleagues, including other nurses, cannot be overemphasized. As a nurse leading care at the bedside, the nurse should be cognizant of their own behavior, remembering that the patient will want to emulate a healthy lifestyle.

This chapter includes narratives, reflections, and questions that will assist readers in understanding the teaching-learning

DOI: 10.4324/9781003586548-7

process as integral to the nurse-patient relationship and to the overall practice of professional nursing. There are many opportunities to learn from these stories. In the novice story, the nurse reflects on her experience as a new graduate nurse. She did not receive teaching or support from the senior nurse, which is an example of a missed opportunity for the novice nurse to learn and practice her nursing skills. She had the inner resources, based on her solid educational experiences, to seek resources on her own. She read the relevant clinical guidelines and sought the support and guidance of nurses who were more willing to teach. She learned quickly how to handle complex cases and used her teaching and learning skills to assist new nurses who had joined her unit, effectively passing along her knowledge. In this experience, the novice nurse learned about leadership, which is not just about the role and authority but also the engagement with other nurses and the willingness to share knowledge. In this reflection, the new nurse learned how not to behave as a role model and was able to turn this negative learning experience into a positive one for herself and her colleagues. There are many resources within the profession that can assist all nurses to engage in civility in the workplace. Take the time to teach other nurses and enhance your own learning.

In the beginner story, the nurse describes her professional learning gap, caring for acutely ill premature babies and needing to teach family members what to expect. She first needed to enhance her own knowledge, including both theoretical/scientific knowledge and the knowledge of the necessary clinical care. Only then could she assist the family in both their understanding of the complexity of the situation for the premature infant but also try to understand their own emotions. The nurse describes the powerful impact her professional knowledge had on her own professional development and the emotional support she was able to provide to family members.

In the proficient nurse story, the nurse describes her professional development in learning to be a charge nurse and progressing to a role as a clinical instructor. She identifies her self-directed learning and teaching of other nurses, culminating in receiving a DAISY Award for her role as a clinical instructor. The "teach-back" method of teaching and learning is a core component of this story and the author's teaching-learning methodology, an approach that serves nurses well in teaching other nurses and patients and families.

The competent nurse story was directly related to the need for patient education following a traumatic health crisis. In this case, the patient's diagnosis was rare, and the nurse had to enhance her own learning to teach the patient and family members. The nurse used all the resources available to her to both teach the patient and the other nurses about the diagnosis that was uncommon. This self-directed learning serves as a key component of her competency as a professional nurse.

The expert nurse story emanates from years of experience in professional nursing practice and leadership roles as well. This expert nurse describes the value of intentional communication in teaching other nurses, both by example and through professional teaching-learning experiences. The same can be said of intentional communication in our teaching and learning experiences with patients, families, and other clinicians. There is a wide range of opportunities to teach others, both formally and informally. This story illustrates both informal and formal teaching and learning experiences.

The nurses' stories of the families' role of teaching and learning to both patient care and nursing professionalism are reminders of these foundational elements in our nursing professional behaviors. Teaching and learning are constant components of the nursing experience, embedded in all that we do as professional nurses.

Teaching and Learning Narrative: Novice

Narrative by Madeline Pavlovich, BSN, RN

I am a registered nurse with a Bachelor of Science in Nursing. My nursing career began working for two years in the Cardiovascular Intensive Care Unit (CVICU) and obtained my Critical Care Registered Nurse (CCRN) certification during that time. During my time there, I had the privilege of holding leadership roles, including serving as a charge nurse and orienting new nurses and nursing students. After two years, I ventured into ICU travel nursing, completing assignments in the Cardiac Care Unit (CCU) Neuro ICUs at various hospitals.

Leadership and professionalism are two distinct yet interconnected concepts. I view leadership as the positive influence one has on those around them; the ability to inspire and guide others toward a shared vision or goal. True leadership transcends professional boundaries; it involves using influence, creativity, and decision-making skills to navigate challenges and foster growth in any setting. Professionalism, on the other hand, is about how you carry yourself. It is the embodiment of a commitment to a set of standards, values, and behaviors that reflect dedication to excellence, integrity, and respect within a field. For me, professionalism is about maintaining focus on the responsibilities and expectations of the role, and it is a key component of effective leadership.

As a new graduate nurse in the CVICU, I was assigned to care for acute post-cardiac surgery patients. I was in a position where I was often taking care of the sickest of the sick. Patients would fly in from all over the world to receive cardiac surgery from our physicians, and I had the honor and responsibility of taking care of them after their procedures. To describe the environment as intense was an understatement, and I was eager to learn, but the reality was far from the supportive environment I had hoped for. The senior nurses were intimidating, often making snide remarks about my lack of experience, calling me "stupid" or saying that I wouldn't last through orientation. I would go home crying almost every day during my first year from feeling bullied and inadequate. They didn't foster learning, and instead of offering guidance, they seemed to enjoy watching the new grad nurses struggle. I vividly remember all the new grad nurses being shoved into a room to settle a fresh case while the senior nurses parked their chairs outside the room, laughing as we struggled, something that was a frequent occurrence on our unit, sometimes happening multiple times in a shift.

I constantly reflect on a day during my orientation period when my patient suddenly began to deteriorate almost out of nowhere. One minute they seemed fine, and the next minute they were unconscious with a blood pressure reading lower than imaginable. I was overwhelmed with fear, unsure of how to manage the situation. Once we had stabilized the patient, the senior nurse that was orienting me that day offered virtually no teaching, but plenty of criticism, screaming at me that the patient's deterioration was my fault and that I was the one that almost killed them. I felt alone and inadequate, and remember going home that evening questioning whether I had chosen the right profession.

Despite the lack of support, I knew that I had to push through. I sought out resources on my own, reading up on clinical guidelines on my off days and practicing my skills with the few nurses that were closer in age to me who were willing to teach. Over time, I grew more confident in my clinical judgment and learned how to handle complex cases. My clinical judgment improved, and I became more efficient in making snap decisions when an acute situation arose.

At the end of my first year, a whole new lot of new graduate nurses joined our unit, and I was assigned to orient one of them. I recognized the same look of fear and uncertainty in her eyes that I once had. This was my chance to break the cycle of bullying and create a supportive environment that I had longed for. I took her under my wing, sharing my experiences and offering guidance whenever I could. I made it a point to foster a culture of learning, where no question was too small, and no mistake was met with harsh judgment.

Over the next few months, I watched her confidence grow. She became more competent in her clinical skills, and I could see the relief in her eyes knowing she had someone to rely on. Today, she is in school to become a certified registered nurse anesthetist (CRNA) just like me. After becoming comfortable and confident in her abilities as an ICU nurse, she had the courage to take the leap of faith to apply for CRNA school and pursue her dream of becoming a CRNA. Reflecting on my journey, I realized that the hardship I faced as a new grad nurse had taught me invaluable lessons about leadership. It was about more than just being clinically skilled; it was about caring for my colleagues, fostering an environment where they could thrive, and being the leader I wished I had when I started.

Through this experience, I learned that leadership isn't just about authority; it's about compassion, patience, and the willingness to uplift others. The senior nurses had taught me what not to do, and in turn, I became a mentor to those who came after me, ensuring that they would have a better experience than I did.

From this experience, I recommend that those in leadership roles or with more experience in a challenging environment actively foster a culture of learning and support for new nurses. Instead of perpetuating negative cycles, use your position to guide, mentor, and uplift others. Small actions, like offering encouragement or taking the time to answer questions, can make a significant difference in a new nurse's confidence and development. Additionally, be mindful of the impact of your communication and behavior, as they shape the workplace culture and influence how new nurses grow into their roles. Cultivating an environment that values both clinical excellence and emotional support not only benefits individual nurses but also improves patient care and strengthens the team as a whole.

Reflection

The bullying and negative culture this nurse author found herself in is abhorrent and, unfortunately, a potentiality of working in any environment. The bravery and leadership this nurse author displays when seeking out self-directed educational and empowerment opportunities are incredible. The behavior of her colleagues on the unit should be reported immediately to nurse leaders so the negativity and "hazing" can be eradicated. We live in a culture where safety is crucial, and the senior nurses who did not offer help in the scenario described above do not exemplify the code of ethics we all subscribe to as nursing professionals. It is our responsibility and privilege to care for others and each other. If activities such as this are not reported, we are allowing this negativity and unsafe behavior to continue and be replicated for future generations of nurses.

As nurses, our role is to constantly educate and reinforce our patients, families, communities, and colleagues. Remaining up to date with the current best practices, policies, and guidelines through professional organizations and peer-reviewed journals, while also staying current with what is happening in the political realm to understand how these practices, policies, and guidelines affect the entire human healthcare landscape, is paramount to being a successful nurse. How can we do our best in teaching others if we are not constantly learning ourselves? Ask yourself, do you know *why* we do things in a certain order, whether it be an assessment, dressing change, or bedside procedure? Remain curious and diligent so you are the most prepared to be the best role model and educator for all populations.

This nurse was curious and remained steadfast in the pursuit of knowledge so she could be the best for her patients and ultimately her colleagues to grow the next wave of nursing professionals. In nursing, we must be open to constant learning and be open to learning from one another.

A potential question related to unsafe and/or negative behavior in the workplace that exemplifies the leadership principles we all must subscribe to may be:

A nurse witnesses a senior nurse colleague bullying a student nurse on the unit. The best response from the first nurse is to:

- **Ask the senior nurse colleague why they are behaving in this manner.**
- **Tell the senior nurse colleague that their behavior is unprofessional, can lead to unsafe or poor patient and colleague outcomes, and that the student nurse deserves an apology.**
- **Immediately inform the nurse manager of the negativity in the unit.**
- **All of the above.**

All of the above would be the best course of action for this scenario. Seeking to understand why the senior nurse colleague is behaving in this manner can open a more nonthreatening conversation regarding bullying and negative behavior in the workplace. Being direct with the senior nurse colleague about why the behavior is unacceptable and standing up for the student nurse is also appropriate and can help regain the confidence and trust of the student nurse. Lastly, informing the nurse manager of the bullying culture that may be present on the unit may allow a non-blaming opportunity for a reset and recommitment to shared values.

Teaching and Learning Narrative: Beginner

Narrative by Latina Jenkins, MSN, RNC-NIC

My nursing career began as a new graduate from a Virginia nursing school, returning home to New Jersey. After passing the NCLEX-RN Licensure Examination, I aimed to secure a nursing position in the Neonatal Intensive Care Unit (NICU). After multiple interviews without an offer, I began to feel discouraged. People advised me to try a different unit and reapply to the NICU after a year, but deep down, I knew exactly where I wanted to begin my nursing career. After months of waiting, I was finally offered a position on a NICU team. As a new grad in the ICU, the experience was far from easy—my orientation was tough, and the pressure to be perfect often left me in tears after shifts. During this challenging time, I had to push myself. My grandmother, who is also a nurse, sensed my struggle and gave me the simplest, yet most powerful, advice: "you wanted this, you deserve this, fight for it." With this guidance in mind, I successfully completed my orientation and became a NICU nurse.

As a new nurse fresh off orientation, I was often assigned to care for complex patients. One experience that profoundly impacted my nursing journey was caring for a micro-premature baby, a baby who was born at only 23-week gestation. Working in an ICU, where every day is fast-paced and unpredictable, the challenges of caring for such a fragile infant were immense. I constantly balanced tasks like drawing labs, administering fluids, and staying on top of all the little details while trying to keep the family informed and supported. In my focus on ensuring the baby's comfort and learning their needs, I realized the parents were struggling with the emotional roller coaster of the Neonatal Intensive Care Unit. It became clear that supporting the family was just as important as caring for the baby.

When caring for these fragile patients, I made it a point to involve the family in the child's care in small, meaningful ways—whether it was guiding them through a diaper change or encouraging them to engage in skin-to-skin contact. I wanted all patients' families to feel empowered and connected, despite the overwhelming uncertainty of the NICU. Although medical advancements have increased the survival rates for 23-week premature babies, it's always a tough battle. This specific patient spent many months in the NICU before finally being discharged home. To this day, I continue to receive updates from the family and am happy to reflect that the former 23-weeker is now a 12-year-old young athlete.

These experiences of caring for acutely ill premature babies taught me how important it is to bridge the learning gap and connect with families during the most difficult times. Teaching and empowering the families to become more involved and seeing a strong family bond grow through small, everyday interactions helped me realize that nursing is not just about the physical care we provide but also includes the emotional support and clinical teaching for the families. Time spent in the NICU can be filled with challenges, but the journey can sometimes lead to a hopeful and happy outcome. Witnessing the shift from doubt to resilience, both in those I support and within myself, is deeply rewarding. These experiences reinforced how vital compassionate care and emotional support are in nursing. Moments like these are powerful reminders of the profound impact we can have through medical care and providing comfort, guidance, and hope when needed most.

The journey to providing exceptional care for a preemie in the NICU isn't easy, but each challenge offers invaluable lessons. With dedication and perseverance, you'll continue to grow as a nurse, building the skills that help you excel and guide and support patients and their families through their own challenges. So, when you think about giving up, remember "You wanted this, you deserve this, fight for it."

Reflection

This author's narrative showcases how, through her inclusion of the family in seemingly small caring tasks for their fragile baby, she empowered the family to take a more active role in the baby's life and ultimately helped the baby flourish to be successfully discharged home. The author may not have realized the gravitas of what teaching new parents how to hold a 23-week-old baby or how to change a diaper or how to soothe and caress their new little one can do. The simple act of teaching the parents these many tasks helped the parents cope and ultimately empowered them to own their situation and move forward through the difficult time.

When delivering education for patients and families, a best practice is to utilize the "teach-back" method. This framework is when the clinical nurse teaches the patient/family and then asks the patient/family to teach the clinical nurse back. The thought is that if one understands a concept or task well enough, they should be able to teach the same concept or task to another.

A potential question related to patient teaching may be:

Your patient and family are ready for discharge from the Neonatal Intensive Care Unit after being admitted for over two months. The following question from the family prompts you to understand that more discharge teaching is necessary. Select all that apply.

- **"Can we stop using the feeding tube now that we're going home?"**

- **Is it okay to call the Physician's Office with more questions?**
- **"Is it okay to skip some of the medications if my baby seems fine?"**
- **If the baby has a fever over 100.4 degrees Fahrenheit, we should call the physician – correct?**

The first answer regarding the feeding tube suggests the family may not fully understand their baby's need for the feeding tube and requires further education on feeding protocols, weaning processes, and follow-up care. The third answer regarding the medications suggests the need for further education on medication administration and ensuring the medications are taken throughout the entire prescription duration. This should trigger the clinical nurse to deliver more education on the importance of the baby taking their medication and how it impacts the baby's recovery. Calling the physician's office is appropriate with additional questions, as is escalating a fever above 100.4 degrees Fahrenheit.

Teaching and Learning Narrative: Competent

Narrative by Mary Grimes, MSN, RN, CCRP

From a young age, I understood the value of good health. I was passionate about helping others achieve wellness. I knew that I wanted a career where I could help people become physically fit and become autonomous with their personal health. I obtained a Bachelor's Degree in Physical Education with a concentration in Adult Fitness. I completed two internships as part of my education. Both internships were in cardiac rehabilitation. I was fascinated. The nurses who ran these departments were integral in helping patients make healthy lifestyle changes. I knew that with my exercise science background, a nursing degree would help me achieve my career goals. I went back to school and obtained my nursing degree. Over the course of my 31-year nursing career, I worked in many different specialties, including telemetry, ICU/CCU, Special Procedures, Endoscopy, and Cardiac Rehabilitation. I returned to school and obtained my BSN degree and then my MSN with a concentration in Population Health. I have thoroughly enjoyed every aspect of my nursing career.

I have a story to tell that encompasses the importance of teaching and learning. This is the story of a young married mother of two young children. She has a job in NYC where she works in fashion. Since the pandemic, this patient had been working from home on Fridays. She was sitting at her desk working and suddenly started to feel unwell. She felt discomfort in her chest and knew something was wrong. Her husband was also working from home that day. She called out to him for help. Her husband found her on the floor, barely responsive. He called 911. This young woman experienced ventricular fibrillation arrest on the way to the hospital and was resuscitated. She arrived at the emergency room, where care continued. She was diagnosed with spontaneous coronary artery dissection (SCAD) requiring emergent left ventricular assist device (LVAD) placement and transport to a higher acuity hospital.

She was my patient for cardiac rehabilitation. I performed her initial assessment and program orientation. This patient's experience was life-threatening and life-changing. She went from being a wife, mother, and high-profile fashion professional to being a survivor. She was scared but also grateful to be alive. My part in this patient's care was equally important as all of the other team players in her care. Cardiac rehabilitation was the perfect avenue for her to regain her confidence and become autonomous in her healthcare. The cardiac rehabilitation team provided her with a safe environment for improving her heart's function. This patient was able to improve her ejection fraction with exercise and no longer was required to wear a life vest. She was able to meet people with heart disease and develop new friendships. Cardiac rehabilitation provided her with education to reduce cardiac risk factors.

As a nursing professional, I recognized that the SCAD diagnosis was very uncommon. I researched SCAD and created a short PowerPoint presentation. SCAD was defined along with the risk factors for SCAD. I also discussed implications for exercise prescription in SCAD patients. This presentation was presented in a journal club to help nurses in cardiology and cardiac rehabilitation care for SCAD patients according to evidence-based practices.

Eventually, this patient was recognized in a special ceremony at our hospital due to her efficient and complete recovery. All team members gathered, including the ambulance team, emergency room nurses and doctors, cardiac catheterization team, and the cardiologist who cared for her. I was also present at the ceremony. We were there to honor and celebrate a special person who made it through a serious condition with grace and gratitude. This represents the care, compassion, and professionalism of healthcare professionals. I am proud to be a nurse.

Reflection

It is amazing how resilient the human body is and that through dedicated education delivered by highly committed healthcare professionals, patients with advanced complex medical diagnoses are able to recover and lead full lives. This author revealed that even as an expert working in a niche, specialized field such as cardiac rehabilitation, a familiar diagnosis presented a challenge. This author was not confident about what SCAD is and how it affects patients in the short and long term. The author took a deep dive into the topic and created an educational program for her colleagues and patients after recognizing that learning had to occur for her to be a successful nurse and patient advocate. This self-directed learning inspired confidence in herself as a nurse and confidence in her patient to own her situation and drive a successful recovery after what was possibly the scariest moment in this patient's life.

A potential question related to this scenario is:

A client is being admitted to a cardiac rehabilitation center. Which of the following best describes the action of the nurse upon admission:

- **Prepare the patient's admission packet, including the identification bracelet.**
- **Identify pertinent health history and assess any learning gaps, limitations, and needs.**
- **Receive any patient valuables and deliver them to a locked safe.**
- **Collect paperwork for the patient's medical record.**

While all answers may be part of the admission process, some of these tasks can be delegated to interprofessional colleagues. The most important action the primary clinical nurse can perform is to identify the patient's health history and assess the learning gaps, limitations, and needs, as this will help direct how the nurse delivers care and which focus areas are crucial. This will help the nurse create a learning plan and establish outcomes while this client is in the nurse's care.

Teaching and Learning Narrative: Proficient

Narrative by Gwendolyn Logan, BSN, RN

I have been an RN for over 20 years and started my career as a nurse for survival and temporary purposes. I was divorced with a bachelor's degree in Zoology, which served me no purpose, and I was a stay-at-home mom for five years. The following few years, I struggled with five menial jobs and was struggling to make ends meet. How did my life become so low? My mother and grandmother were nurses, and they encouraged me to get my associate degree in nursing at a community college to support myself and my son. At first, I balked, but then I realized I needed to do something to survive, so I reluctantly went back to college and got my associate's degree with the mindset that this career choice was going to be temporary until I could figure out what I really wanted to be in life.

Once I graduated in 2003, I knew I wanted to start in the intensive care unit (ICU) and became the very first ICU nurse resident. I had heard about "nurses eating their young" mentality and was a bit timid with the very seasoned nurses in the ICU. To my surprise, it was the best environment with the most supportive, intelligent, and loving people who taught me the foundations of being a good ICU nurse. I learned from so many of them and was a full-time staff member for five years, then went per diem for another ten years. I have also worked in an off-site ambulatory surgery center affiliated with the hospital. There, I learned to become a charge nurse and found my leadership style to be more democratic style, where everyone's voice was heard and valued.

I went back during these years to obtain my BSN because of the trend and push from the hospital to have more RNs to have their BSN degree. It was all completely paid for by my hospital, which I appreciated. It was then that I started to think about what advanced degree I would like to have. After much research, I decided to become a certified registered nurse anesthetist (CRNA) for the reason that I can still provide my ICU nursing skills and care to patients receiving anesthesia. I value this core of nursing because I can give my best to one person at a time.

Upon receiving my BSN in 2019 and talking with multiple program directors across the country, the consensus was that I needed to explore other ICUs at a Level 1 teaching hospital and expand my knowledge base for CRNA school. I did some travel nursing and ended up as staff at Duke Hospital at the start of the pandemic. In the pursuit of being accepted to CRNA school, I would research and try to find different ways to stand out as a qualified candidate. Most program directors wanted extraordinary above and beyond the typical GPA of 4.0 and were looking for candidates who did more than just work in an ICU and had good grades. The representative candidates could have done community work, specialized certifications in their field, been published, been actively involved with committee work at the local, state, or national level, and obtained awards in nursing

I had done some precepting at Duke Hospital in the cardiothoracic unit, and at first, I was extremely nervous because I didn't feel like I really had anything to teach as I was still learning myself. I had no prior experience in teaching a new nurse, and I took an online course through the hospital about developing the necessary skills to become a great preceptor. My first person was a nursing student from the Duke School of Nursing, and she wanted to become an ICU nurse, and I was able to connect with her. We had such a great connection, I feel, because we were honest about the care we were providing. We had a comfortable, non-judgmental, open, respectful relationship where we were able to work so fluidly together. Whenever she was with other ICU nurses, she explained she did not have that comfort with learning and experienced lateral violence, again, the philosophy of eating the young mentality. She talked with the clinical coordinator, Big AL, about our experience, and he sought me out to discuss if I would consider teaching as a clinical instructor for the school of nursing, teaching new nurses on the floors. I initially declined because I was intimidated and not confident that I could actually teach them anything. I really believed that. After another semester, Big Al approached me again and was able to convince me through his persistence and charm how important and valuable I would be to the new nurses.

I started working as a clinical instructor at the School of Nursing at Duke in the winter, summer, and fall semesters of 2022. I worked hard to create a safe, psychological space for the students and I to explore and learn together. The students worked as a team, and we created a bond that was inclusive, respectful, and fun. The students learned from me as I was at the bedside, for example, teaching them how to do a proper head-to-toe assessment, how to suction a trach patient, and how to give medications through a G-tube. I really enjoyed seeing them light up with excitement each week as we met and performed safe, quality patient care together.

Many times, I would prepare a topic and hand out resources (ex., learning how to measure ECG strips and interpret them), and then we would practice on the unit. Other times, I let the students express what they wanted to talk about. We allowed for mutual sharing and self-directed learning. In the spring of 2023, I received the DAISY Award in my role as a clinical instructor from the nursing students at the Duke School of Nursing. I was surprised and honored by the award. Receiving this award made me proud of having the courage to teach others even when I was unsure of myself. It also allowed me to learn about leadership styles, to give back to the profession that I grew to love, and to hopefully change the next generation of nurses to be kind to each other in our profession.

Reflection

This author highlights the importance of believing in oneself and having the confidence to help others grow through learning. We become experts in our field without even realizing it. This author was unknowingly an expert and eventually was recognized as an expert and a successful, and an appreciated teacher. As nurses, we are leaders. People look to us to inspire and forge the next generation of nurses…so it is imperative we believe in ourselves to own this responsibility.

A potential question related to teaching others is:

As a clinical instructor, you are teaching student nurses how to suction a tracheostomy. Which of the following teaching methods would help the student nurses understand how to perform this bedside procedure?

- **Show the students a step-by-step tutorial video.**
- **Demonstrate the proper methods in a classroom and have the students perform the procedure after you.**
- **Ask one of the more experienced student nurses to perform the procedure.**
- **Give the students a handout on the procedure.**

Using the demonstration and performance method is similar to the "teach-back" method discussed in the previous narrative reflection. Demonstrating the procedure in a controlled setting, such as a classroom, allows the student nurses to feel safe in a non-threatening, non-acute setting. Ensuring the students perform the procedure after watching the demonstration certifies that the student nurses synthesized the main points of how to safely suction a tracheostomy. A video and handout can be nice supplemental learning materials, but until the student nurses perform the procedure themselves, the clinical instructor should understand that the learning process is not complete.

Teaching and Learning Narrative: Expert

Narrative by Nicolette Fiore-Lopez, PhD, RN, CENP, FAONL, FAAN

I have been a nurse for nearly 47 years. My professional journey has been rich and rewarding. I spent the first half of my career at a major academic medical center in New York City, most of it in Critical Care, beginning as a new graduate, clinical educator, and several supervisory roles. The second half of my career has been spent in community hospitals, over twenty years as a Chief Nursing Officer.

Clinical competence in nursing as a prerequisite for assuming a leadership role should continue to be supported for entry-level positions. As we know, nurses are trained differently and use their clinical competence and training as they develop leadership skills that allow them to effectively navigate nursing's role in the healthcare landscape. Nursing leaders represent their staff at all levels of the organization and, as such, must maintain their connection to those who are providing direct care to patients, regardless of the setting, or those who may be educating nursing students. Additionally, nursing leaders must recognize that they are modeling the way for the next generation of leaders and educators. This serves as the background for the narrative that follows.

Shortly after graduating with my baccalaureate in nursing, I returned to school for a master's degree in nursing education. I had a phenomenal critical care nurse educator, and I wanted to be just like her: she was smart, she was energetic, and it was quite apparent that she had a passion for her work. Several years later, I realized that as much as I liked to teach, I also wanted to move up in the organization. When I looked around, I made the decision that I did not want to be a Director of Nursing Education. I did, however, want to be the Director of Critical Care, so I secured a nurse manager position.

Fast forward to two years ago, when I received an email from a former coworker who I also considered a friend; in fact, we car-pooled together to work. Her husband was a fireman for the Fire Department of New York (FDNY). She wrote to tell me that she had recently attended a retirement party for one of her husband's coworkers. During his retirement speech, he thanked the spouse of another fireman, who he said was his clinical instructor during his RN program years ago. Afterwards, my coworker connected with the former clinical instructor. Unbeknownst to either of them, when they first started to talk, they had worked together in the critical care unit where I had also worked. They began discussing the names of nurses who they worked with, and my name was mentioned. This former instructor said that, of course, she remembered me and also shared that I was the reason why she sought her master's degree in nursing education and became a clinical instructor. Her exact words were "I wanted to be just like her." Reading that email that day literally brought tears to my eyes. The cycle had repeated itself: I wanted to be just like my clinical instructor, and I had pursued the education, just like this nurse wanted to be just like me.

As professionals, we have frequent discussions about the impact of what we do daily. But when we have those discussions, it is usually about the tangible impact of our work: quality and financial data. We rarely, if ever, discuss how our work may be viewed by others who may wish to follow in our footsteps. I am frequently reminded that my words are repeated and, at times, taken out of context, so I try to choose them wisely. I do not remind myself enough that it is also how I may or may not respond to issues and other daily or long-term events that color perceptions of leadership by those who will be the next generation of leaders. This story underscores that it may be the intangibles of our work, how we appear to others, that may have the most lasting impact.

Reflection

Once again, we see the power of human connection through nursing. This author was inspired by others to become a nurse and pursue higher education, and didn't realize that, in turn, this author was inspiring others to do the same. We make an impact on our patients, families, colleagues, and communities without even realizing it. Possibilities for continued education and advanced learning exist all around us. Make sure that as you grow your career, you consider the educational opportunities within and outside your organization. You never know how you will be inspiring others to do the same.

Chapter 8

Other Narratives from Professional Leaders at the Bedside and Beyond

DOI: 10.4324/9781003586548-8

Narrative by Susan Weaver, PhD, RN, CRNI, NEA-BC

My experience as an RN consists of majority compliments, barring exceptionally difficult or demanding patients. I feel rewarded and proud to be a collaborating RN. I consider being a bedside nurse as a privilege to me. We come across so many different cultures, perspectives, personalities, attitudes, inspirations, and life learning 1:1 opportunities than any other profession. Especially when I work three shifts in a row as an RN, the same patient and their family members become like my own family members. I feel the bond and connection getting stronger each day I take care of them, which makes me experience the hospital as my 2nd home.

I love my profession and my patients. Seeing a smile on their face(s) makes me more confident to leave a positive impact on their health beyond the medical treatment. When fully pleased with my care for them, patients at times offer me a monetary gift as a token of gratitude. But, I always redirect them kindly to bake something sweet and leave it at the nurses' station, sip room with their room number so that the staff can recognize, acknowledge, and enjoy their love-full experience. For the staff, what else can be more rewarding than this!!

As an RN, I provide my duties as a collaborator between patients, physicians/residents, consulting physicians, interdisciplinary teams such as PT/OT/Speech therapist/respiratory therapist/dietician, dialysis team, imaging modalities, social worker, transport, and so on. Because, guess what!! For everyone, the contact key person is the patient's nurse who is in charge of the patient for the day.

As an RN, I provide a physical, emotional, and holistic approach to my patients. Because of an illness, when my patients' own capabilities are on decline, I serve as a savior for them by providing quality care with compassion and safety. I also advocate for my patients to maintain their autonomy.

I have performed my duties as a charge nurse on the unit also. During this time, I have experienced the support, love, teamwork, and respect of my colleagues more closely. Trust me, wearing multiple hats on the same head is not a piece of cake. It certainly demands a lot of skills, critical thinking, emotional intelligence, prioritizing and shifting gears, deep breathing, focus, tolerance, and patience beyond physical strength every single day. And, I will say that it has reformed my own life as an individual as well. Having dual degrees as a healthcare professional has made me feel and experience the difference I am able to make in a patient's life. And thus, my mission in life to serve mankind and give back to society has been fulfilling.

Narrative by Nader Alnomasy, PhD, RN, AGNP-BC

I have had the privilege of being a trailblazer in many aspects of my life and career. I am currently an assistant professor at a university in Saudi Arabia, as well as an adjunct assistant professor at a US university. My educational journey has taken me from Saudi Arabia to the United States, where I was the first in my family to study abroad. Each step of my journey has shaped my leadership philosophy, which is deeply rooted in persistence, perseverance, and a passion for advancing the nursing profession both nationally and internationally.

Leadership, to me, is the ability to inspire, guide, and support others toward achieving shared goals. It is about leading by example, building connections, and being proactive in the face of challenges. Professionalism in nursing is about upholding the highest ethical standards, committing to lifelong learning, and contributing meaningfully to the growth of others. Both leadership and professionalism require confidence, trust in oneself, and the persistence to overcome obstacles.

My journey was filled with challenges that tested my perseverance. I was the first in my family to become a nurse and to travel abroad for my education. When I arrived in the United States to prepare for the NCLEX, I was shocked by the difference in the level of critical thinking and knowledge expected of me. At that time, I felt alone in a new country with a new culture, new language, and new educational standards. I worked hard to prepare for the NCLEX while simultaneously improving my English by attending language school. This period taught me that persistence and perseverance are the keys to shaping one's future.

Despite these challenges, I passed the NCLEX and completed my English studies. From there, I pursued a master's degree as a nurse practitioner, a role that was unfamiliar and challenging to me. Yet, it was a step I was proud to take because I wanted to return home and use this knowledge to build and strengthen the nursing profession in Saudi Arabia. I continued my educational journey, earning a PhD in nursing at Case Western Reserve University, where I had the opportunity to work with top scholars in the field. These experiences sharpened my understanding of how to lead, innovate, and think critically about the profession of nursing.

One of the most transformative experiences in my career was joining a post-doctoral fellowship program. I learned how to lead by example, build connections, and proactively shape my future as a global leader in nursing. I was fortunate to work with living legends in the nursing world who taught me the tools I needed to validate my contributions and make meaningful impacts on the field.

Throughout my career, I have learned that persistence and confidence are essential to success. After working hard as a nursing faculty member, where I taught fundamentals, medical-surgical nursing, leadership, and pharmacology, I found myself full circle—teaching students how to prepare for the NCLEX, a journey I once found so difficult. By 2023, I was promoted to assistant professor at a School of Nursing in Saudi Arabia. Looking back, I realize that my path from a struggling student to an expert instructor proves that no obstacle is insurmountable with persistence and self-belief.

One of the key lessons I learned through my journey is that leadership in nursing is not just about influencing change at a local level, but also internationally. My passion for leveraging AI in healthcare, particularly in nursing, has driven me to pursue health informatics at the University of Pittsburgh, where I learned essential skills such as Python programming and working with SQL databases to manage large datasets. I was involved in various AI-driven projects and contributed to publications, poster presentations, and competitions such as datathons. These experiences have reinforced my belief that modern nursing leaders must expand their contributions not only in clinical practice but also in the realms of education and technological innovation.

Embrace persistence and perseverance: There will always be challenges in your journey, but persistence will push you forward, and perseverance will help you rise above them. Continue to grow and adapt: Whether you are learning a new skill, adapting to a new culture, or taking on a new leadership role, growth comes from embracing change and pushing past your comfort zone.

Lead by example: Show others that leadership is about creating an environment for success, not just for yourself but for those around you.

Leverage technology and innovation: The future of nursing is intertwined with advancements in AI and healthcare technology. Equip yourself with the necessary tools to lead in this evolving landscape.

In conclusion, my journey from a new nurse in Saudi Arabia to a leader and educator in both Saudi and American institutions has taught me that leadership is a continuous process of growth, learning, and adaptation. By fostering a passion for education, technology, and innovation, I believe we can shape the future of nursing and create a lasting impact on the global healthcare system.

Narrative by Deborah Dillon, DNP, RN, CRNP, ACNP-BC, CCRN, CHFN, FAANP, FAAN

My definition of leadership and professional advocacy comes from a clinical experience while I was a nurse practitioner in a private practice and was a member of a hospital credentialling committee. In this community (2012), the role of the nurse practitioner (NP) was just being recognized in the hospital setting. Although the credentialling committee was for allied health professionals, it had limited nursing representation. The predominant members were physicians who felt it their role to define the scope and practice of NPs. I volunteered to be on this committee to represent the voice of the NP. I was the only community, non-hospital employee on the committee (non-paid, if I can add).

The allied health credentialling committee met monthly at 7:00 a.m. Not my preferred time, but they did have "wonderful coffee." At each meeting applications were reviewed for various advanced practice nurses (APRNs), including clinical nurse specialists, nurse practitioners, and certified registered nurse anesthetists. At one particular meeting I recognized the name of one of my former family nurse practitioner (FNP) students on the list for requested privileges. She was requesting privileges to work on the inpatient neurology service and function as an NP member of the stroke team. I had this student in the transition to practice course, in which scope of practice, the 2008 Consensus Model, and licensure and certification are addressed. I was immediately disappointed that the student did not grasp the content of the course related to population foci and scope of practice. Understanding the 2008 Consensus Model, which delineates the population foci of each NP specialty, I knew this FNP was requesting privileges that were outside of her scope of practice. It seemed easy enough to me to state my opposition and decline the request for privileges. This is when I first realized the challenge that I was up against. The physicians all voted to approve the privileges as requested. The Chief Nursing Officer and another NP also declined to approve the request. This was essentially nursing versus medicine.

It was now my opportunity and responsibility to advocate for the NP role and provide education on the 2008 Consensus Model. It was felt by the physicians that the collaborating physician could provide the necessary education and training. Meeting one ended. Item moved to next meeting agenda.

At the following month's meeting I provided evidence-based documentation on the specifics of the Consensus Model as well as articles by experts in the nursing field discussing the implementation of the model and the legalities associated with practicing outside of one's scope of practice. I endured humiliation by the Committee Chair as he said, "Thank you for your opinion." I clarified for the minutes that it was not my opinion but the opinion of nursing experts and that I agreed with the literature. I was also questioned on my vote, and I had to request that the minutes reflect my opposition to the requested privileges. It was clear from this meeting that the understanding of the NP role was that of "a nurse is a nurse is a nurse" mentality. Another vote was taken with the same results as the first. Vote tabled until the next meeting.

In the interim more opposition occurred. I was accosted in the physician parking garage by the FNP's collaborating physician, a neurologist. He wanted to know why I was not approving the privileges as requested. He queried what it would take to get her privileges approved. I explained the scope of practice difference for the FNP versus adult-gerontology acute care NP (AGACNP). This information did not satisfy him. He assured me he would provide all the necessary training and supervision. I thanked him graciously for offering to help acclimate her to the role, but that would not change her scope of practice. When I explained about a post-master's certification in an AGACNP program, I was accused of trying to protect my role as an acute care NP and not allow other NPs to be credentialled.

At the next monthly credentialling meeting, the pressure on me was ramped up even more. The neurology collaborating physician went to his physician colleagues on the committee and put pressure on them to get the NP's privileges approved. I again defended my original stance on scope of practice, using patient safety concerns, potential litigation, and again the Consensus Model, as well as prior documentation that had been presented. I continued to be supported by my nursing colleagues. Once again, the vote was tabled until the next meeting.

I grew increasingly uneasy as the next meeting approached. It would be easier to "cave" and allow the privileges to be approved. Change is difficult, and this is still an "old boys club." I was experiencing this firsthand. Many physicians were approaching my collaborating physician with concerns regarding my stance. I even had a private meeting with the hospital's legal counsel to garner support. He did not want to go up against medical administration. My privileges were being closely monitored.

The day of the meeting had arrived. As I was getting a cup of that "wonderful coffee" I was approached by the Chief Medical Officer (CMO) who said, "Deb it is with humblest apologies that we have put you through this. Don't worry, I'll take care of this today." This statement definitely piqued my curiosity. The CMO started the meeting outlining everything I had been presenting for the last several months. He felt we could not and should not approve the requested privileges. The vote was taken, it was unanimous, and privileges were declined. It was interesting that when the CMO speaks, everyone agrees. The recommendations then go to the Medical Executive Committee for approval.

I felt wonderful and vindicated. My leadership, education regarding the role/scope of practice, and persistence paid off. I learned to advocate and not succumb to bullying by medicine. I demonstrated leadership for the NP profession. I now knew what being victorious felt like.

My success was short-lived. Two weeks later the Medical Executive Committee met. The Medical Executive Committee consists of physicians and the Chief Nursing Officer (she has a seat at the table, but no vote). One of the physicians on this committee was the neurology collaborating physician. The vote by the credentialling committee was overturned at the Medical Executive Committee – privileges granted.

I resigned from the credentialling committee as I could not be a member of a committee that would be legally held accountable for privileging and that those recommendation could be overturned. Ironically, at the same time, I received my "thank you for your service letter," and a new committee member would be appointed.

I learned many lessons from this experience. NPs must advocate for each other. Even though the NP role has been in existence for over 50 years, the educational process as to our role and scope will be lifelong. You are in a leadership position just because you are a nurse or an NP. Nursing must have a voice and a vote in all policy, whether it is at the federal, state, or local level. From personal experience I understand fully what the saying "If you're not at the table, you're on the menu" means. Nursing can't just be at the table, but they must have a vote as well. As an educator in nursing, I continue to stress scope of practice and the implementation of the Consensus Model. Finally, this experience also reinforced that it does take approximately 15 years to get research implemented into practice. The 2008 Consensus Model was still considered "new" information in the 2012 experience.

I moved into academia in 2015. I am happy to say that in 2017 I saw a position posting for an AGACNP at this hospital. Change does eventually occur, but not necessarily on your timetable. Be persistent and stay strong.

Narrative by Bianca Inclema, MSN, RN, CCRN

I have been a Registered Nurse since 2018. I have held several RN positions in various specialties throughout that time. I began my nursing journey as an adult post-op medical/surgical nurse, which was an amazing experience and taught me the fundamentals of nursing (time management, bedside manner, prioritization, delegation, etc). About two years later, in 2020, I wanted to challenge myself in a completely different way and became a pediatric trauma ICU nurse. This was a major transition and learning curve as our unit quickly became an adult ICU during the COVID-19 pandemic. The ICU was an experience I will never forget – the very good and the very bad. This position taught me how to critically think and connect the dots between disease processes, while managing care for a patient in a critical setting. I will forever be grateful for that time in my life to be a critical care nurse and the patients that I have closely cared for. I had the opportunity of being a charge nurse overnight, and that helped me realize I wanted to further develop my leadership skills and see other ways that I could lead a team. I furthered my education and obtained my MSN in advanced leadership, while becoming a nurse manager on a pediatric step-down unit. Getting a degree in leadership while learning how to become a leader in real time was a unique process, but an invaluable experience. Today, I currently oversee a pediatric step-down unit, a pediatric infusion center, and a pediatric cancer center. I learn something new every day in this role, and every skill I learn is another stepping stone helping me to achieve my goals. I chose to pursue a DNP – because I was hungry for more. A whole new set of doors opened when I began my doctoral degree, which lit a flame within me to push myself to the next level. I would also love to publish my own book/s one day – inspiring newer nurses/nursing students to maximize their experiences as a nurse and explore all that this profession has to offer (which, in my opinion, is limitless).

I often get asked to define what a leader is and what professionalism means to me. I am a believer that leadership and professionalism often overlap. A leader who demonstrates professionalism sets a strong example for their team, while professionalism in leadership involves guiding others with integrity, competence, and respect. Both qualities are essential for fostering a productive, ethical, and respectful work environment, ultimately contributing to individual and organizational success. In my humble opinion, a true leader is someone who embodies several key qualities and practices that go beyond simply holding a position of authority.

Prior to my current role as a Patient Care Director, I assumed that leadership was going to be a breeze and making change would be easy, but was I wrong! In fact, being a nurse leader has been one of the most challenging roles I have had throughout my time as a nurse. It takes grit, strong character, emotional intelligence, and patience to be successful in the role of a nurse leader. In my first year of being a nurse leader, I was heavily focused on the daily tasks (staffing, finance, quality, patient experience, etc) and completing those tasks well, in a timely manner. While those are all vital components to a nurse leader's job description, I found the hardest and arguably the most important responsibilities were related to building relationships, managing conflict, and communication. I can remember one specific experience where there was conflict within one of my own departments – among some of the interdisciplinary team, which led to tense relationships and overall decreased unit morale. This type of dynamic in the workplace is considered toxic and inhibits the development and growth of a healthy work environment. I needed to address the situation right away. After doing a little fact-finding, I learned that the entirety of the conflict was due to a small miscommunication between individuals. The solution was to bring the teams together, validate their individual feelings/experiences, and collaboratively come up with a plan to create proper communication channels that could aid in the prevention of future conflict.

The lessons that I learned as a novice nurse leader and the recommendations that I have for you are to be proactive when conflict arises and lead with a solution-based mindset. Another lesson I have learned over my time as a nurse leader would be to seek advice from a mentor or another leader with a strong foundation of experience in your area of specialty. In this situation, I was able to reach out to my director supervisor and learn strategies of how best to initiate the process of building the team dynamic through managing conflict. As a leader, you don't have to know it all – you are not expected to, but you should know your resources well, and I feel strongly that this applies to all nurses, no matter where they are in their journey. Speak up – ask for help – but most importantly, be kind to yourself. You are changing the world.

Narrative by Cheryl Hoover, MSN, RN

Ever since my first pediatric rotation in nursing school, I have wanted to be a pediatric nurse. When I graduated, I began my career on an adolescent unit. A lot of my patients were newly diagnosed oncology patients. I considered myself to be a compassionate nurse who was extremely patient-focused. What I did not realize was that I had a lot of room to grow. I would often internally judge the parents for giving into their children or letting them have whatever they wanted.

I have always heard that your experience shapes who you are, but I never thought they would shape who I was as a nurse and leader. I feel I am a good pediatric nurse, but once I became a mom, I became a great pediatric nurse. I finally understood what the parents were going through and how scared my patients were. I remember my first day back from maternity leave with my first child. I had transferred to the operating room, and my patient was having cardiac surgery. The mom came back to the operating room with her infant son. As I walked her back to the preop area she began to cry. For the first time I truly understood what this mom was going through. She had just handed over the most important thing in her life to us. It was our responsibility to make sure we took the best care of her child. To care for her child as if it was our family member.

I have never forgotten this moment and how it defined my practice as a pediatric operating room nurse. Every patient I take care of, I treat them as if they were my own. If I would not want something for my child, it is not good enough for anyone else's.

In the operating room there are two roles for a nurse. You are either the circulating nurse or the scrub nurse. I enjoy both roles, but when I am the circulating nurse, my satisfaction comes from taking a scared child from their parents and using games and songs to bring them back to the operating room without them even knowing they just left the most important person to them or that they are going into surgery.

I have continued this way of thinking as a leader in the pediatric operating room. I mention it often to my staff. Our mantra is to treat our patients as if they were a family member. This way of thinking is not just for the frontline staff. We drill it into every employee. This includes the staff that cleans the operating rooms, transports the patients, and sterilizes the instruments.

When I am interviewing potential staff, I always share that the one trait every staff member in our department displays is as a strong patient advocate. Every person in our operating room realizes the importance that they do. They know that our patients do not have a voice when they are in the operating room. We are that voice. We make sure they are receiving the best care from everyone.

Orientation in the operating room can take up to a year. This can get frustrating for seasoned staff who have to do all of the off-shift obligations until new staff are completely oriented. On the off shift, our operating room only has two staff members in-house. Whenever staff come to me frustrated about new staff not moving through orientation faster, our discussion is always around one question: would you want your child/family member taken care of by staff not fully oriented? The answer is always no.

I do not believe you have to be a parent to give the best nursing care. That is the journey I needed to take for me to realize that although I am taking care of the patient, that patient has a lot of people that love them who also need my attention and compassion.

Narrative by Geoffrey Stepnick, BSN, RN

I am a student registered nurse anesthetist who previously served as a bedside nurse at a major academic medical center in a specialized intensive care unit for five years. I grew up in a family of healthcare providers: my parents a doctor and a nurse, with a grandparent and a stepparent also nurses. I saw the sacrifice and challenges that these positions demanded throughout my childhood, which became an undeniable part of my being. Despite this, I thought that I wanted to follow my own path with a career that I believed to be more relevant to my curiosities at the time: computer engineering. Shortly into my college education, I quickly realized that this perceived interest was not what I had envisioned, lacked fulfillment, and not truly something that I wanted to do for my whole life. Almost simultaneously, I was thrown further into a tailspin by a personal health crisis. This required a formal withdrawal from my studies, and as my recovery dragged on, I ended up abandoning my previous goals. I became unfocused, seeking some sort of fulfillment in what I did or wanted to do – to no avail. This search involved trial and error – mostly error – where I took an eclectic mix of community college courses. I was not fully invested in any of them and increasingly unsure of myself, resulting in my educational performance suffering significantly.

After long resisting the thought of working in the healthcare field, my father invited me to see the environment he worked in every day and what went on there: the operating room. Following several such visits, I took keen interest in a person who made everything there possible by providing the conditions for surgery to proceed: a nurse anesthetist. Something clicked, and I decided that this is what I wanted to do. The road to get there would not be easy. Looking back, my personal journey towards becoming a leader started here; in order to be accountable for others, I first had to become accountable to myself. This turned out to be a long and arduous task: I had yet to fulfill any of the requirements to seek entry into a nursing program. I also had to prove that my unfocused state and its negative impact on my educational performance was something I had moved beyond. This took longer than I had hoped – to the tune of several years.

When it finally came time to apply to nursing programs, my initial attempt was met with denial, which could have been the end of my journey. However, I remained determined and I didn't give up. I continued to work to demonstrate that I was a worthy candidate, becoming involved in volunteer work at hospitals and retaking courses – even ones that didn't involve health or nursing. I began to understand that fixing the mistakes of the past was hard work, but that becoming accountable to these problems was making me more resilient, more driven towards my goals. The following year, I was given the opportunity to prove myself I had hoped for, in a baccalaureate nursing program, and I fully invested myself to that end. The result was graduating with a near-perfect grade point average. However, my successes were not limited to my efforts in the classroom or singularly focused on myself; my clinical performance and interactions with patients were highly regarded by instructors, peers, and patients alike. My classmates also started to do something that was surprising to me: they looked to me for guidance. I was invested in their success as well as my own, and welcomed the sharing of knowledge and experiences, that we all might become better providers. Following graduation, I was fortunate to obtain a position in an ICU. My actions now carried significant weight, as lives were now on the line. I put everything into learning as much as I could in order to provide the best care I could to patients and to become an invaluable part of an effective team. This was not an easy environment to exist in, and even though I still had much to learn, I realized that other nurses were soon looking to me as a mentor. Like before, I sought to share knowledge, as well as provide support and encouragement for my colleagues: nurses, residents, and others. Building them up sought to make us all better. I was becoming a leader in a way that fit my personality: as an undercurrent that was recognized, but quietly and efficiently lifted others up.

After several years, I finally decided that it was the right time to continue my journey towards my ultimate goal of becoming a nurse anesthetist. I knew from the beginning of my journey that admission to a graduate program would be one of the biggest hurdles to overcome, despite all that I had gone through. My first attempt had shades of my efforts to get into nursing school: I was offered an interview but not selected. Again, I remained persistent and aimed to prove that I had learned and grown from my past mistakes and experiences. No matter the outcome, I was proud of the work I had done to better myself, finally finding purpose. The following year, I was given the opportunity I had worked towards for nearly a decade. Today I sit here, nearly halfway through this program, again giving all of my effort to prove that I have something important to offer and belong here. I've learned that we can all make a difference, no matter where we've come from or what we've done. I seek to give others that opportunity where I can, much like the opportunity that was given to me. That might just be the spark needed to help someone do something great.

Additional References

Clisbee, D., Beierwaltes, P., & Eggenberger, S. K. (2019). Reducing digital storytelling implementation barriers in nursing education workshops. Journal of Continuing Education in Nursing, 50(9): 411–416. https://doi.org/10.3928/00220124-20190814-07

Fitzpatrick, J. J. (2018). Teaching through storytelling: Narrative nursing. Nursing Education Perspectives, 39(2): 60.

Fitzpatrick, J. J. (2021). Narrative nursing: Empowering nurse leaders. Nursing Administration Quarterly, 45(4): 324–329. https://doi.org/10.1097/NAQ.0000000000000486

Fitzpatrick, J. J., Rivera, R., Walsh, L., & Byers, O. (2019). Narrative nursing: Inspiring a shared vision among clinical nurses. *Nurse Leader*, 17(2): 131–134.

Halverson, K. L. (2020). *A narrative approach to understanding the experience of becoming and being a nurse: Professional identity formation among new nurses* [Doctoral dissertation, Queen's University]. Retrieved July 7, 2023 from http://hdl.handle.net/1974/27548

Kim, M., Lee, H., Kiang, P., & Allison, J. (2019). Development and acceptability of a peer-paired, cross-cultural and cross-generational storytelling HPV intervention for Korean American college women. Health Education Research, 34(5): 483–494. https://doi.org/10.1093/her/cyz022

Mancini, M. A. (2019). Strategic storytelling: An exploration of the professional practices of mental health peer providers, 29(9): 1266–1276. https://doi.org/10.1177/1049732318821689

Murphy, R., & Higgins, A. (2018). The complex terrain of peer support in mental health: What does it all mean?, 25(7): 441–448. https://doi.org/10.1111/jpm.12474

Phillips, C. S., Volker, D. L., Becker, H., & Davidson, K. L. (2021). Storytelling through music to improve well-being in oncology nurses: A feasibility study, 44(6): 473–481. https://doi.org/10.1097/NCC.0000000000000836

Peterson's. (2019). *Master the NCLEX RN exam (1st edition).*

Rennick-Egglestone, S., Morgan, K., Llewellyn-Beardsley, J., et al. (2019). Mental health recovery narratives and their impact on recipients: Systematic review and narrative synthesis. *Canadian Journal of Psychiatry*, 64(10): 669–679. https://doi.org/10.1177/0706743719846108

Schaer, J. M., Campbell, L. A., & Thomas, L. J. (2022). The first line of prevention: A public health nursing advocacy video. Public Health Nursing, 39(3): 677–682. https://doi.org/10.1111/phn.13013

SchoenhoferS., & Boykin, A. (2023). Storytelling: A strategy for caring connection in creative nursing leadership. Nurse Leader, 20(4): 349–351.

Timpani, S., Sweet, L., & Sivertsen, N. (2021). A narrative inquiry of storytelling: A learning strategy for nursing students to reflect on their interactions with patients. Reflective Practice, 23: 232–245. https://doi.org/10.1080/14623943.2021.2013191

Troy, L. M., & Kietzman, K. G. (2016). Enhancing evidence-based public health policy: Developing and using policy narratives. Journal of Gerontological Nursing, 42(6): 11–17. https://doi.org/10.3928/00989134-20160516-04

Tussing, T. E., Giakas, D. A., & Mulder, C. (2023). Storytelling: A legacy continuing to connect theory and practice. Nurse Leader, 20(4): 361–365.

Wadsworth, P., Colorafi, K., & Shearer, N. (2017). Using narratives to enhance nursing practice and leadership: What makes a good nurse? Teaching and Learning in Nursing, 12(1): 28–31. Elsevier Ltd. Retrieved July 7, 2023 from https://www.learntechlib.org/p/198520/.

Wang, L., Wu, D., Wu, S., et al. (2022). The effect of narrative nursing intervention on shame in elderly patients with bladder cancer after ileal bladder replacement: A cohort study. Computational and Mathematical Methods in Medicine: 4299919. https://doi.org/10.1155/2022/4299919

Wang, Y., Xu, Y., & Li, J. (2022). Effect of narrative nursing combined with thinking map health education on parturient self-efficacy and neonatal nursing ability. Computational Intelligence and Neuroscience: 8466797. https://doi.org/10.1155/2022/8466797

Zhang, L. H., Meng, H. Y., Wang, R., Zhang, Y. C., & Sun, J. (2021). Application of narrative nursing in the families of children with biliary atresia: A retrospective study. World Journal of Clinical Cases, 9(34): 10557–10565. https://doi.org/10.12998/wjcc.v9.i34.10557

Index

Acquired immunodeficiency syndrome (AIDS), 151
Adult-gerontology acute care NP (AGACNP), 198, 200
Advanced practice nurses (APRNs), 197
Against medical advice (AMA), 54–55
Agency for Healthcare Research and Quality (AHRQ), 87
Ambulatory nursing, 115
American Nurses Association (ANA), 4
Anesthesiologist, 68–69, 71
Assessment, diagnosis, planning, implementation and evaluation (ADPIE), 136–137, 141

Cadaver transplants, 91–92
Cardiac Care Unit (CCU), 169, 179
Cardiac rehabilitation, 179–181
Cardiovascular Intensive Care Unit (CVICU), 143, 169
Caring, 15–16
  Ashley Kovacs (Competent), 33–36
  Dorothy Chan (Expert), 43–46
  Gloria Gomez (Beginner), 25–31
  Jill Cohen (Novice), 18–24
  Mallory Potondi (Proficient), 37–41
Certified Nurse Operating Room (CNOR), 67
Certified registered nurse anesthetist (CRNA), 171, 184
Chemotherapy Nurse, 107
Chief Nursing Officer (CNO), 18, 159, 187, 198, 200
Clinical judgment, 47–48
  Andriy Melnychenko (Proficient), 63–65
  Competent, 59–62
  Jennifer Ezeokobe (Beginner), 53–57
  Juliann Altman (Expert), 67–73
  Kerri Hensler (Novice), 49–52
Communication and documentation, 74–77
  Competent, 91–94
  Expert, 99–102
  Katherine Babcock (Proficient), 95–98
  Kelly Varga (Beginner), 85–88
  Maria Molnar (Novice), 79–83

Compassionate care, 34
Confusion Assessment Method (CAM), 147
Consensus Model, 200
COVID-19 pandemic, 16, 43–44, 107–108, 112, 132, 155, 201
Critical Care Registered Nurse (CCRN), 169
Critical thinking, 47
Cultural and spirituality, 103–105
  Cait Hogan (Novice), 107–113
  Deborah Lindell (Expert), 127–135
  Melanie Walter (Beginner), 115–118
  Molly Jackson (Proficient), 123–126
  Peter Stoffan (Competent), 119–121

De-escalation techniques, 41, 56

Empirical knowing, 4
End-of-life care, 29, 112
Esthetic knowing, 4
Ethical knowing, 4–6
Extracorporeal Membrane Oxygenation (ECMO), 143, 145–146

Facial drooping, 88
Family nurse practitioner (FNP), 197
Fire Department of New York (FDNY), 188

Geriatrics Resource Nurse, 107

Hematology/oncology unit, 139
Holism, 103
Hypertensive crisis, 64

Immune Thrombocytopenia Purpura (ITP), 139
Intensive care unit (ICU), 16, 49, 53, 79, 91, 183
International Council of Nurses (ICN), 4, 6
Interprofessional team, 23, 30, 59, 71, 87, 95, 145–146
Intracranial pressure, 61–62

Kenya, 130
Kidney transplant surgeries, 91

Leadership, 20, 25–26, 33, 53, 143–144, 155, 169, 171–172, 187, 194–195, 197, 200–202
Left ventricular assist device (LVAD), 180
Licensed Vocational nurse (LVN), 33
Living transplants, 91–92

Medical Executive Committee, 200
Medical intensive care unit (MICU), 63, 147
Medical-surgical unit, 152–153
Memento box, 16, 33, 35

National Council of State Boards of Nursing (NCSBN), 13
National Patient Safety Institute (NPSI), 72
Neonatal Intensive Care Unit (NICU), 175
Neurosurgery, 59–60
Non-governmental organization (NGO), 127
Nurse practitioner (NP), 79, 197
Nursing
  Benner's Model, 7
    levels of proficiency, 11–12
    six domains, 8–9
  Bianca Inclema, 201–203
  Cheryl Hoover, 205–206
  Deborah Dillon, 197–200
  emotional intelligence, 7

Geoffrey Stepnick, 207–209
holistic nature of, 4
Nader Alnomasy, 193–195
patterns of knowing, 4–7
Quality and Safety Education for Nurses (QSEN), 10–11
six integrated processs (NCLEX-RN), 13
Susan Weaver, 191–192
ten provisions, 5–6
workshops, 2–3
Nursing process, 136–138
Akeliah Robertson (Competent), 147–150
Angela Prestia (Expert), 159–164
Emily Hanna (Beginner), 143–146
Katelynn Dharap (Novice), 139–142
Mary Joy Garcia-Dia (Proficient), 151–157

Oncology Resource Nurse, 107
Open reduction and internal fixation (ORIF) surgery, 51

Palliative Care, 123
Pediatric Intensive Care Unit, 26
Pediatric step-down unit, 200
Perioperative nurse, 20
Personal knowing, 6–7
Plan, Do, Study, Act (PDSA), 136
Post-anesthesia care unit (PACU), 68–69, 91
Pre-operative nurse, 99
Professional development educator, 43
Professionalism, 25–26, 28, 53, 55, 107, 111, 143–144, 147, 167, 169, 193, 202
Prognosis, 97–98, 108, 118–120, 124
Psychiatric diagnosis, 56

Quality and Safety Education for Nurses (QSEN), 10

Rapid response team, 50–51
Rehabilitation hospital, 18, 20

Self-directed learning, 167, 181, 185
Skin Care Resource Nurse, 107
Social determinants of health (SDOH), 125–126
Spinal cord unit, 18, 20–24
Spontaneous coronary artery dissection (SCAD), 180
STAT medications, 152

Teach-back method, 177, 186
Teaching-learning process, 165–167
Gwendolyn Logan (Proficient), 183–186
Latina Jenkins (Beginner), 175–178
Madeline Pavlovich (Novice), 169–174
Mary Grimes (Competent), 179–182
Nicolette Fiore-Lopez (Expert), 187–189
Team Strategies & Tools to Enhance Performance and Patient Safety (TeamSTEPPS), 87
Teamwork, 18–19, 30, 154, 192
Thrombocytopenia, 141–142
Turkana County, 127–128, 130–131

Ventricular Assist Devices (VADs), 143
Ventriculoperitoneal (VP) shunt surgery, 59

World Health Organization (WHO), 7

Young pediatric oncology patient, 26–28

For Product Safety Concerns and Information please contact our EU
representative GPSR@taylorandfrancis.com
Taylor & Francis Verlag GmbH, Kaufingerstraße 24, 80331 München, Germany

www.ingramcontent.com/pod-product-compliance
Ingram Content Group UK Ltd.
Pitfield, Milton Keynes, MK11 3LW, UK
UKHW022118190926
475702UK00013B/1517

* 9 7 8 1 0 3 2 9 5 0 8 9 1 *